PHILIP
GREEN
WAY

THE UNAUTHORIZED GUIDE TO DOING BUSINESS THE PHILIP GREEN WAY

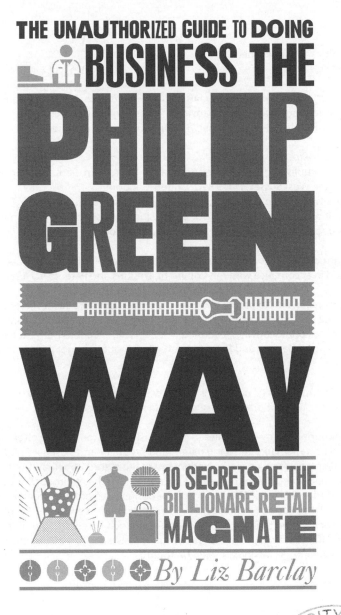

10 SECRETS OF THE BILLIONARE RETAIL MAGNATE

By Liz Barclay

CAPSTONE

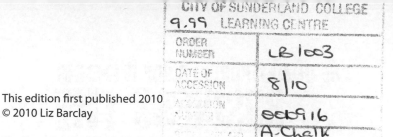
This edition first published 2010
© 2010 Liz Barclay

The Unauthorized Guide To Doing Business the Philip Green Way is an unofficial, independent publication, and Capstone Publishing Ltd is not endorsed, sponsored, affiliated with or otherwise authorized by Philip Green.

Registered office
Capstone Publishing Ltd. (A Wiley Company), The Atrium, Southern Gate, Chichester, West Sussex, PO19 8SQ, United Kingdom
For details of our global editorial offices, for customer services and for information about how to apply for permission to reuse the copyright material in this book please see our website at www.wiley.com.

Library of Congress Cataloguing-in-Publication Data is available

9781907312366

A catalogue record for this book is available from the British Library.

Set in Myriad Pro by Sparks (www.sparkspublishing.com)
Printed in Great Britain by TJ International Ltd, Padstow, Cornwall

CONTENTS

ACKNOWLEDGEMENTS

Philip Green is an instinctive entrepreneur who owns 12% of the UK's clothing retail sector. It's been fascinating learning about his rise to fashion retailing dominance and working out how he does business the Philip Green way.

Because it's difficult to get people to talk about Green's way of doing business, with friends and foes reluctant to say anything, this book owes a huge amount to my two contributing analysts who offered their opinions of his business practices and retailing acumen. Thank you both.

I'd also like to say thank you to my researcher Hannah Matthews and the team at Capstone for giving me the opportunity to write this book, and for their support and guidance. And thank you to my business partner Tony Fitzpatrick for his patience with my neglect of other projects while I've been working on this book.

I include at the back of the book a list of all the references used in that research – too numerous to mention here. The journalists who've written about the entrepreneur over the last 25 years have contributed greatly with their insight into the man as well as his business. The unauthorized biography *Top Man: How Philip Green Built His High Street Empire* by Stewart Lansley and Andy Forrester is terrifically well researched and written. It goes into the details of his career, which isn't the purpose of this book, so if you want to know more – much more – about the life and times of Philip Green, read this, it's a great story.

THE LIFE AND TIMES OF PHILIP GREEN

'The unsweetened version of Alan Sugar and a fashion retailing genius.'[1]

Fashion analyst

Take a walk down your local high street and have a look. There's sure to be at least one Philip Green-owned fashion emporium – a Topshop, Dorothy Perkins, Wallis, Evans or Burton, maybe a Topman or Miss Selfridge. Some towns have several, plus another of Green's brands – the department store Bhs. His Arcadia empire is privately owned by the Green family and is the second biggest in the fashion sector in the UK after Marks & Spencer. So what does it take to become one of the UK's most successful entrepreneurs and one of the biggest names in UK retailing?

Surely there can be few people left in the UK who don't know who Philip Green is. His picture is rarely out of the papers, often with glamorous celebrities on his arm such as Kate Moss and Naomi Campbell. His business dealings have been dissected and reported on for the past 30 years. His personal fortune is regularly speculated on and his birthday parties are the subject of the gossip columns. His yacht, jet, homes, tax status, son's bar mitzvah, wife's talent for interior design, mother's business acumen, employees, business partners, takeover bids, profits, debts and dividends have all been scrutinized and made the front pages. But for all the millions of words that have been written about him, he's still a man who defies categorization.

THE CLOTHES MAKETH THE MAN?

He has been called the unsweetened version of Alan Sugar and heavy-handed; he claims to be determined, focused and forthright, and that he never bears a grudge. He's renowned for not mincing his words, and the people who have an opinion seem fairly equally divided between those who think he's the best thing retail has ever seen and those who wouldn't give him house room.

It's hard to dispute that he's a multi-talented entrepreneur and one of Britain's most successful retailers, but there's also been acres of print given over to the debate about whether he is a wheeler and dealer who buys and sells businesses for the good of his own pocket.

Green has kept alive or revived many existing brands that were looking decidedly sickly before he threw his weight and financial muscle behind them. In his more triumphant moments, he has been hailed as the finest retailer of his generation and one of the best business brains in the UK; at other times in his career he has received criticism for taking too much money out of his businesses and under-investing. He claims to increase profits through efficiencies in operation costs and the supply chain, although those on the receiving end have said this felt more akin to turning the lights down, cutting costs and squeezing his suppliers. In the past, his critics have been quick to point out that he is not so effective in building sustainable businesses that attract more customers, but his success with Topshop has proved them wrong.

He's a man who's hard to pin down. For every friend he has a detractor, for every critic a supporter. There is simply no consensus to be found on any aspect of the man and his career. So who's opinion to believe? I can't make that judgement. What I can say is that when I met and interviewed Philip Green for a BBC radio documentary recently, I left his office as a fan.

Yes, he's blunt and forthright, and it's easy to see how some of his employees and associates could find his manner difficult to deal with. But he's willing to admit he doesn't get it all right all of the time and that he, along with every other retailer in the high street, has to keep reviewing his business tactics and strategy in light of new and increased competition, and adverse economic conditions.

I felt he was realistic; driven, determined, focused, possibly ruthless, impatient, according to staff insiders sometimes bad tempered, determined to do things his way – but above all, realistic. His friends claim he is the way he is because that's what it takes to succeed in the tough retail environment; his detractors say that's no excuse for his sometimes overbearing behaviour.

When I asked him what the biggest mistake he'd made in his career was he told me it had been talking to me for the last hour. Rude? I don't think so: just his way of being humorous, and he did share his sweets with me – always the way to my heart. He certainly wasn't the difficult person I'd been warned to expect and I came away feeling he was tough but fair.

To balance my views I've enlisted the help of two analysts to give me their take on the maestro's performance over the past couple of decades. They're a retail analyst and a business analyst with, between them, 60 years of high street experience.

SETTING OUT

Philip Green was a Croydon-born, middle class Jewish boy who left school at 15 without a single qualification. It's become a bit of a cliché in the business world – it's almost de rigour to leave school as soon as allowable having achieved as little as possible academically. It's probably fairly common among entrepreneurs because even at school they have the traits of the entrepreneur – restlessness, impatience, a desire to be making money, a low tolerance threshold, the vision to see themselves elsewhere – none of which translates into good marks in the classroom.

Now in his late 50s, Philip is number six on the latest *Sunday Times Rich List,* up from ninth in 2008 despite – or perhaps because of – the recession. He's estimated to have around £3.8 billion in his personal coffers, for family futures or for his next high street acquisition. Impressively, he's reported to have made his first billion quicker than anyone else in British history and, once the first was made, the others swiftly followed. So how did Philip Green build his business empire? How did he get from an academically challenged teenager to the owner of the Arcadia Group, which runs about 12% of the UK clothing market?

It's fairly easy to chart Green's march along the high street from 1992. Most of his recent ventures have been the subject of intense press and media interest. But it's less easy to unearth the exact detail of his early and less successful enterprises. It has also been difficult to obtain many details of how he runs his operations, and his personality still remains something of an enigma.

THE CHILD IS THE FATHER OF THE MAN

Philip Green was born in 1952 on 15 March (known by every Shakespeare scholar as the Ides of March – a day to be feared!). His parents, Simon and Alma Green, already had a daughter, Elizabeth, and were an enterprising, well-to-do Jewish family. Both ran small businesses: his father ran electrical businesses and rented out TV sets, and his mother ran laundrettes and petrol stations. TVs and washing machines were the stuff of dreams for many people in the 1950s, so the Greens were ahead of their time. They also owned properties through a small property company. Philip has called them 'business obsessed', and his attention to detail is likely to have been either inherited or learned from them.

Philip was sent to an academic boarding school. Being away from the family at boarding school is traumatic for most children but it must have been much more so when Philip's father died of a heart attack in 1964 when Philip was 12. The adult Philip has been described as difficult, always looking for affirmation and confirmation from his peers that he's the best despite his protestations that he doesn't care what others think. A psychiatrist may look to the early death of his father for the source of some of those traits. Having been sent away to school at nine, he'd had little time to form a relationship with his father and his relationship with his mother was closer. He said in an interview with the *Daily Mail* in 2004 that 'she's been my biggest influence and my role model. She was the strong one, good at business and very determined.'[2]

Whatever the impact of his father's early death, Philip Green seems to have had few friends at school afterwards and he certainly wasn't academic. He spent his weekends and school holidays helping his mother with her businesses. At the petrol station he cleaned windscreens, changed oil and earned tips from the customers – and seems to have acquired the taste for both business and money. Sitting in a classroom can't have been easy for a boy who was learning about business outside of it and who was naturally inclined to be out there making money.

But academic failure often spurs people on to make their mark later. It could be that their position in the school league table leaves them with a desire to be better than the classmates who look down on them and gives them the determination to make it big in some area of life. Green came from a business background and many entrepreneurs with business in their blood, who leave school with few qualifications, attribute a degree of their success to that desire to thumb their noses at their former classmates.

APPRENTICESHIP

When Philip left school in 1968 his mother encouraged him to go into business. He may have had no qualifications and started at the bottom, but he was from a relatively well-off business family that provided him with some money and contacts. He was left some money by his father. Having learned a lot from his parents about running businesses, he saw the advantages of owning properties that can be used for raising business finance, and his mother used her connections to get him an apprenticeship in the wholesale shoe trade.

Fashion was undergoing a real revolution at the time Green started work. People, particularly young people, wanted something new and fresh. They wanted 'fashion' instead of 'clothes'. Prices were falling too. People wanted to buy more, cheaper items. It was no longer enough to have one dress or jacket, but there wasn't a great deal more money with which to build up a decent wardrobe, so bargain hunting was the order of the day. Retailers were beginning to look for clothes made outside the UK to save costs and bring prices down.

The shoe company Philip was working for did business with Hong Kong and so he had an early insight into how that type of business operated. At first he worked in the warehouse and as an errand boy, running around London with samples to show prospective buyers. He certainly started at the bottom and worked his way right to the top. After about four years in the business, Green was allowed to sell at shoe exhibitions. He did a deal on 40,000 pairs. His boss bet him £5 that he wouldn't get the order. He did. It was his first order and his boss paid the money ... although Green found himself having to hand it back a few weeks later when the order was cancelled! The shoe trade was a great grounding for Green and may well have had a strong influence on his approach to business today.

On his 21st birthday, Green joined the family property company, Langley Road Investments, but the fashion business was where he wanted to be. He was starting to understand the industry and it was well suited to his restless entrepreneurial mind, since it was an industry that was changing at a fast pace. Even then he was always on the lookout for the next trend and working out what customers wanted to spend money on. The money he'd been left by his father and a business loan launched the would-be entrepreneur into the business world.

THE FUTURE'S BLUE

Denim was becoming popular in the early 1970s and Philip Green saw its potential. Early on he was proving that he had an eye for future trends and was willing to grasp opportunities. He was one of the first to source jeans from Hong Kong.

Throughout the 1970s and into the 1980s he ran several businesses, usually with his mother, that were ultimately unsuccessful. He had a shop called Bond Street Bandit; a business called Cupcraft that went bust in 1982; another, Tarbrook, a clothing importer and wholesaler, was wound up a year later, with debts of £239,000 and assets of just £436; in 1983, he became a director of Buzzville, a women's clothing manufacturer 50%-owned by his mother, but again it went into voluntary liquidation; and there was the Joan Collins Jeans Company, which was set up in 1981 but, thanks to a lack of interest in Joan Collins, went under a year later.

Green has been reported many times to have said that he never managed to start anything successfully himself – but as the next phase of his career was to prove, just because he hadn't started up a successful business didn't mean he couldn't take over and successfully turn around failing businesses and make them work. It was this ability that was to become the trademark of his earlier career and make his original fortune.

Most successful entrepreneurs don't make money out of their first, second or even third ventures. They're likely to have a few under their belt before they happen upon the one that makes their name and fortune. Most people don't know about running a business until they're in business and then they learn as they go along. Philip Green was no different and he certainly did learn, throughout the 1970s, some vital skills that he used to great advantage later; how to do deals with suppliers and how to work out what customers want to buy and at what price.

By the time Green had been in the rag trade for 15 years, he hadn't made any real money. He'd had several businesses wound up by receivers, an experience that can be very disheartening for many and ultimately drive them out of business. But Green was made of sterner stuff and he certainly had no intention of giving up. And just to prove that nothing goes to waste in business, it was his experience of business failures that gave him his next opportunity. Green was just getting started.

TURNING THINGS AROUND

Over the next few years, denim and failing businesses were a winning combination for Green. He concentrated in rescuing and turning the businesses into viable operations to sell on. The owner of the ailing business Bonanza Jeans, a clothing wholesaler, contacted Green because of his experience with companies facing liquidation. Green raised the money to keep Bonanza afloat, took ownership of two-thirds of it and left a grateful owner with one-third of a viable business. The money came from mortgages on properties owned by the Green family property business and a mortgage on the assets of Bonanza Jeans in Taunton. Green had learned the value of being able to raise money quickly and how owning property was the key to being able to raise much needed cash. He also knew that owning a third of a viable, growing business is much more appealing to most business people than owning 100% of a bankrupt business, so he could make money out of these deals. The empire was beginning to grow.

Green then went about recovering debts owed to Bonanza from a company called Jean Jeanie, another denim retailer. As it turned out it was ailing too, but Green saw it as another opportunity and bought it too. He told *The Guardian*: 'I could see what had happened … Bad buying, no discipline, no control, old stock, indecision, time-wasting, corporate thinking … [I] got the business back to breaking even in four months.'[3]

And so it was after those four months when Green announced that both Bonanza and Jean Jeanie were back in profit. He had restructured, cut out many of the suppliers, bought straight from manufacturers in China and Hong Kong, renegotiated contracts and saved money to refurbish some of the shops. About six months after he got involved with Jean Jeanie, he did a deal worth £7 million with the big British jeans wholesaling company Lee Cooper, repaid Jean Jeanie's overdraft and his debts to the bank, and had money in his pocket. It was hailed as the success story of the 1980s and made Green a fair return on his investments. Lee Cooper set up a retailing arm with Green as managing director. But despite a good salary and the possibility of earning millions of pounds over the following three years, based on company profits, Green didn't enjoy the restrictions of having a board to answer to and left about a year later.

A STUMBLE

Green had earned his reputation as a deal maker and a problem solver. And he'd had his first taste of working with a board and found it not to his liking. But that didn't stop him trying his hand at running a public listed company. In 1988, Green put his problem-solving skills to work on rescuing Amber Day, the fashion business. Green put in a large amount of his own money and became chairman and chief executive. Amber Day acquired 13 Review stores and, in his first year in charge, Review made a profit of £1 million. Green then bought the Woodhouse group in 1989. He was grabbing headlines for Amber Day, relentlessly promoting the company to his contacts and courting publicity. Interest and headlines in the business pages pushed up the share price. The transformation was spectacularly rapid. He restructured, opened new stores and set up licensing deals in Europe.

He twice attempted to acquire Moss Bros but the owners weren't interested. Rumours circulated that he was interested in Next, then Richards, then the Sears Group. His desire for high street domination was evident even then. But recession was around the corner and consumers' spending habits had changed. By the end of the 1980s, spending was falling, and Review and Woodhouse's profits were being hit. Green needed a recession-proof firm to balance the books.

Opportunity knocked when Gerald and Vera Weisfeld, who knew Green well, decided to sell their Glasgow-based discount department chain What Everyone Wants. According to one Glaswegian resident at the time, it was nicknamed 'What Nobody Wants', and would have made today's Primark and pound stores 'look like Harrods in comparison'. It must have seemed an odd fit then with the upmarket Review and Woodhouse chains, but Green saw its potential and bought it for £47 million, adding around £120 million of potential sales and £6 million in profits to the Amber Day group.

While Green was being hailed as a genius and proving yet again that he could spot real opportunities, there were mutterings about the wisdom of one man holding both the chairman and chief executive posts at the expanding Amber Day. (There have been similar questions raised recently of Sir Stuart Rose holding both posts at Marks and Spencer.) Amber Day was a one-man band with Green firmly in control, and it was very much reliant on him.

Amber Day was the second-best stock market performer in 1990, even outperforming Marks and Spencer. Green enjoyed the fruits of his labours with a nice house and cars, and made influential friends. But as the recession took hold and businesses collapsed, fund managers and bankers became choosier – in what and whom they invested.

Green's Amber Day chains were feeling the heat like everyone else. At the beginning of 1992, analysts were forecasting profits of about £15 million for Amber Day – well up on 1991. In June, Green's forecast was that profits would exceed the previous year's £10 million. But the share price had started to fall and went on down. The city was no longer in thrall to its wonderboy. In early August, with the share price at 31p, Prudential – one of Green's biggest supporters – sold its 6.1 million shares at 27.5p. When the profits were announced in September they were £7.5 million and the die was cast. The profits forecast had been substantially wrong and the board accepted Green's resignation. And just to knock a man when he's down, as soon as Green resigned the share price rose by 2p.

ON THE UP

Green's deals after Amber Day restored his reputation and each deal made him richer. He bought Owen Owen, the fifth biggest department store in the UK, which he eventually sold on. He snapped up Mark One, a discount fashion chain for teenagers, when it went bust in 1996 and restyled it MK One. He bought Shoe Express from the Sears Group, followed by the once mighty Sears Group itself, which he split up and sold in profitable parcels. He then bought Bhs, which he kept, and eventually Arcadia. He still owns Arcadia, which of course includes Topshop, and Bhs has been merged into the group so that it now has eight brands.

Green has become an entrepreneur respected by his peers and has been honoured several times by his industry as well as by Her Majesty. He's a celebrity in his own right and a household name.

As with anyone in that position, he's attracted his share of hostility from his detractors – but his dedicated followers, grateful customers, loyal staff and supportive friends love the colourful, dynamic, business-obsessed tycoon.

GREEN'S WORLD

- **1952:** Born 15 March in Croydon.
- **1961:** Goes to Carmel College (a Jewish boarding school, now closed).
- **1964:** Father dies of a heart attack.
- **1967:** Leaves school and works as a shoe importer.
- **1973:** Joins family property investment firm. Sets up first business with a £20,000 loan, importing jeans from the Far East.
- **1979:** Opens first shop in Conduit Street, London. Brings in jeans from Far East. Buys and sell designer label clothes at discounted prices.
- **1981:** Opens Bond Street Bandit in New Bond Street, selling imported designer labels. Launches Joan Collin Jeans to an unenthusiastic public.
- **1982–5:** Several ventures end up in the hands of receivers.
- **1985:** Takes two-thirds of Bonanza Jeans, a jeans supplier in Taunton. Chases up money owed to Bonanza by jeans chain Jean Jeanie. Buys Jean Jeanie. Turns both firms round. Meets Tina (Christina Palos), his future wife.
- **1986:** Sells Jean Jeanie to Lee Cooper. Makes his first million. Becomes Managing Director of Lee Cooper's new retail arm (which he quits in 1987).

- **1988:** Becomes chairman and chief executive of menswear company Amber Day. Owns 17% of the company.
- **1990:** Buys What Everyone Wants for Amber Day for £47 million. Marries Tina.
- **1991:** Chloe Green born.
- **1992:** Resigns from Amber Day after profits lower than forecast with a £1 million payoff. Brandon Green born.
- **1993:** Sells remaining shares in Amber Day for £7/8 million. Buys Parker and Franks discount fashion chain in administration and creates Xception.
- **1994:** Buys Owen Owen.
- **1995:** Bails out Owen and Robinson, closing the jewellery chain and selling off the profitable footwear chain. Buys the Olympus chain from Sears Group (retail footwear and fashion chain) with Scottish friend and entrepreneur Tom Hunter for £1 plus £30 million of debt. Has chest pains and rushed to hospital. Avoided a full heart attack.
- **1996:** Buys Mark One discount chain for teenagers and restyles it MK One. Sells eight Owen Owen stores to Allders.
- **1997:** Buys 185 Shoe Express stores from Sears Group for £8.3 million; 75 become MK One stores.
- **1998:** Sells 110 Shoe Express stores to Stead and Simpson for £20 million. Buys family home in Monaco. Tom Hunter sells Olympus to JJB Sports, making Green a good return.
- **1999:** Buys retail chain Sears UK with the help of Tom Hunter and the Barclay Brothers, and breaks it up. Sells some brands, including Wallis and Miss Selfridge, to Arcadia. Makes huge profit. Launches £7 billion bid for Marks and Spencer. Withdraws.

- **2000:** Buys Bhs for £200 million. Profits are up at the end of year one; trebled by the end of year two.
- **2002:** Bhs worth £1.2 million. Buys Arcadia, which includes Topshop, Wallis and Burton, with backing from HBOS, for £850 million. Celebrates his 50th birthday by taking 200 guests to Cyprus for a three-day long party.
- **2004:** Makes second bid for struggling Marks and Spencer. The Company appoints Stuart Rose as Chief Executive. He and the board fight off the takeover bid. Marks and Spencer would have cost Green around £11 billion. Passes control of Arcadia group to Tina.
- **2005:** Awards himself a £1.2 billion dividend from Arcadia. Buys ten Allders stores. Puts up money for Fashion Retail Academy.
- **2006:** Profits fall at Bhs and Arcadia. Buys Etam; sells some stores and converts others into his own brands; the Tammy brand aimed at younger shoppers sells in Bhs. Appoints Kate Moss to design range for Topshop. Gets his knighthood in the Queen's 80th birthday honours list for services to retail.
- **2007:** Jane Stepherdson quits as Brand Director at Topshop.
- **2008:** Makes a rescue bid for part of the Baugur Group, but lost to other buyers. Buys and sells share of Moss Bros for just over £1 million profit.
- **2009:** Opens Topshop flagship store in New York. Merges Bhs into Arcadia, with Ian Gradiner as Chief Executive. Throws 50th birthday party for Simon Cowell. Sets up a new entertainment company with Simon Cowell.
- **2010:** Another chapter in the Green story unfolds.

HOW DOES HE DO IT?

So what are the business maxims that have taken Philip Green, the teenage rag trade runner to knighted high street mogul, with a multi-billion-pound personal fortune? Like any other experienced entrepreneur, he's done it his way. Without the strictures of a business school education, he isn't confined by it. He's followed his instincts in most cases and he's learned as he's gone along. He's had his share of hard knocks and difficult lessons.

With my retail and business analysts I've endeavoured to look at how Green has conducted his business since things started to go his way and his grip on the high street strengthened. He has traded through several recessions but this latest has been, as it has for most other retail entrepreneurs, a real test of his mettle. And to date he's surviving well. Green is here to stay and he's doing it 'his way'.

1
DO IT YOUR WAY

'I know Green is not everyone's cup of tea and it's certainly not great fun getting on the wrong side of him, but it's hard not to find his sheer enthusiasm and energy for the business of retailing both infectious and endearing.'[1]

Tim Danaher, *Retail Week*

Green and his wife Tina are estimated to be worth in the region of £4 billion; he's reported to have made the fastest £1 billion ever and he awarded himself the biggest dividend in British retail history, in 2005, of £1.2 billion. He has admitted in dozens of interviews over the years that whatever he does, he does it to make money, but he also works hard at being a first-class retailing entrepreneur. And he does it his own way.

Green doesn't have a formal business education, but he has a wealth of experience gleaned from working in the fashion business since leaving school. He has built up skills and knowledge of all aspects of the industry from the sourcing of zips and fabric, through manufacturing and importing, to the shop floor. And at all points he does his business his way – an approach that has made him a vast fortune.

A TOUGH OPERATOR

He has a reputation for being a tough operator, with boundless energy and a formidable temper. He's driven, ambitious and competitive, and likes things done his way. He's a hands-on boss who calls the shots. He surprises his staff by turning up unannounced – sometimes late at night – to check everything in his stores is as he wants it. He has an eye for detail and a feel for what people want. Many find his enthusiasm and passion for business motivating; others complain that he's unpredictable. But he seems to know his limitations; for example, he has admitted in interviews that he's not an expert in teenage fashion and not good on style, but he knows the value of having the right staff to fill the gaps in his own skills.

In October 2009, Green announced that pre-tax profits at the Arcadia Group – which includes Wallis, Dorothy Perkins, Burton and the jewels in the crown: Topshop, Topman and Miss Selfridge – had increased by 13% in the 12 months to the end of September 2009, despite the recession. He appears to own most of the trappings you'd expect a man of his wealth to have, and lives in London and in Monaco.

Green doesn't have a formal business education, but he has a wealth of experience gleaned from working in the fashion business since leaving school.

So how does he do it? A prominent businessman told me recently that he believes Philip Green is that rare thing – an instinctive businessperson who does things unconsciously. 'If you asked him,' he said, 'he probably wouldn't be able to tell you why he does some of the things he does. He just sets his sights on the end goal and heads straight for it, refusing to take no for an answer.' Maybe that's the only way to make the kind of money he's made. If you refuse to take no for an answer – refuse to accept that things can't be done – maybe people are forced to think out of the box, creatively, to come up with solutions in business that they otherwise wouldn't come up with.

The BBC's former Business Editor Jeff Randall reported in 2002 that Green had once said to him: 'You know how you feel about golf – well that's how I feel about retailing.'[2] According to Randall, who knows Green, he has few hobbies apart from the odd game of tennis. His business is his hobby. He does enjoy gambling, as in playing the tables at the casino, but as an entrepreneur he also seems to enjoy taking gambles on businesses that he thinks he can grab from the jaws of failure and turn into successes. In short, Philip Green is passionate about retail and that's probably what makes him so good at it in the eyes of his peers.

TO THE BUSINESS BORN

Being born into a business family probably gave Green a head start. His is not the fashionable rags-to-riches tale that so many entrepreneurs love to trade on and that the public laps up. As I've mentioned, his parents ran their own businesses and Philip helped out while he was growing up. He may not have realized it, but he was absorbing business skills and know-how.

With both parents as business role models, being in business and working for himself would probably have seemed natural. Going into business would probably have been his preferred option. Given his lack of achievement academically, it became his best and perhaps only realistic option for making a living.

As an entrepreneur he also seems to enjoy taking gambles on businesses that he thinks he can grab from the jaws of failure and turn into successes.

So business was a natural way forward for Philip Green and his mother's connections got him his first job with a company of shoe wholesalers. Neither of his parents was in the 'rag trade', but by 1968 – when Philip left school – the rag trade was undergoing a revolution. Fashion was beginning to be glamorous and in demand, but it was the young people who demanded it and then, as now, they needed fashion at prices they could afford. For most that meant at the cheaper end of the market.

Most of the clothes in the UK had been made in the UK until the 1960s, and were relatively expensive, but retailers who wanted to tap into the youth market had to look for ways to keep their prices down. They could buy what they wanted, cheaper, from overseas manufacturers, even allowing for the costs of importing the goods.

The wholesale shoe firm Green worked for when he left school did business with manufacturers in Hong Kong – so right from the beginning of his career, importing from the manufacturers would have seemed to him the most cost-effective way to do things. And he would have learned how to negotiate deals with manufacturers and buyers that kept both sides happy. It was to stand him in good stead and throughout his career Green has done many of his deals directly with manufacturers, cutting out the whole-sale middlemen.

Throughout his career Green has done many of his deals directly with manufacturers, cutting out the wholesale middlemen.

From shoes Green moved to jeans and from there into the fashion trade, which is where most of his business career has been spent. He was lucky in that having a business background and already having some money helped him when he needed to borrow from the banks to get started.

With denim the fabric of the moment, and American jeans very popular but expensive and out of the reach of many young fashion-conscious denim wearers, Green spotted a gap in the market. He brought jeans in from factories in Hong Kong where they were being made much more cheaply. He could spot the designs that people were likely to want and had them made up in Hong Kong. In 1981 he tried out his celebrity-branded 'Joan Collins' jeans. It wasn't one of his better ideas. He may have been an astute businessman, importer and negotiator, but he appears to have failed as a judge of what young people would consider 'cool'. Young shoppers in search of jeans didn't want to be associated with the middle-aged Joan Collins. What had worked well in the States with the actress Gloria Vanderbilt in 1979 failed dismally with Joan Collins, and the jeans had to be sold off at big discounts. The company followed the jeans into obscurity. It was one of a few business set-backs for Green but he always had several other ideas in the pipe-line, so there was no time to wallow in despair – he just bounced back and got on with the next venture.

By the age of 30 Green had shown many of the traits he's still known for today: his ability to do deals, a capacity for bouncing back from setbacks, that sheer enthusiasm and energy, determi-nation, passion and focus, and the ability to spot an opportunity. And the recession of the early 1980s gave him plenty of opportuni-ties – to go into the retail side of the business and challenge the established way of doing things.

GRAND DESIGNS

Green found a lot of shops were closing down as landlords strug-gled to re-let them. Closing shops had to get rid of stock fast and were willing to sell at rock bottom prices. People were buying cheaper clothes and the shops selling designer labels were par-ticularly badly hit. It was another winning combination for Green. He heard about stock for sale from ten shops that were closing down and he bought it cheap. Rather than just sell it on to retailers, he bought a shop in New Conduit Street (a much more upmarket area of London than the wholesale trading area he'd been used to) and sold his discounted designer label clothes from there – to the outrage of upmarket shops around about still open for business.

His next shop was on the even more upmarket New Bond Street. He bought the lease and stock, and sold the lot at knockdown pric-es in a week. He went to Italy for more, piled it high, sold it cheap and had queues in the street. Nothing about his venture made him popular with the surrounding retailers. He was selling high quality, designer label fashion for street market prices from a shop called Bond Street Bandit. That word 'Bandit' just about summed up how his fellow retailers in the street felt about the upstart Green.

At the time the big design houses allowed only exclusive boutiques to sell their clothes, a policy that kept prices high. Green had found a way around it by dealing with people in Europe who were willing to sell him last year's designer label ranges at huge discounts that he could then pass on to the customers. He made headlines and was seen as a champion of consumers. Eventually he found it more and more difficult to get his supplies and profits tailed off. Still, he'd fired a warning shot across the bows of the retailing aristocracy and made a name for himself in the process.

Green is not afraid to take a risk, but it will be a calculated risk.

By the time he called a truce with the designer houses, he had three businesses in liquidation and had been in the industry for 15 years without making any real money. But he wasn't about to throw the towel in and had begun to make a name for himself in trade circles. He got involved in Bonanza Jeans and Jean Jeanie, turning around their fortunes, and began to build a reputation for himself as someone who could see a way through a difficult situation and do a deal that others simply didn't see. His financial fortunes began to change.

DAY OF RECKONING

As explained earlier, Green then concentrated on taking over and turning round struggling businesses. Amber Day was the one that proved a nightmare for Green and had a long-term impact on his career. My retail analyst says:

'I believe he was profoundly affected by Amber Day and sees his own way as the only way to avoid being shafted. Ironically, as much as to be rich, his drive is to be loved and admired – even by the establishment he professes to distain. Consorting with high profile, A-list celebrities looks to me to be but a manifestation of this psyche.'

It's certainly apparent that his experiences at Amber Day left Green determined that his skills were much better suited to running private companies. He's an entrepreneur who runs his businesses on gut instinct. He likes to get on with making things happen and not be hampered by the demands of shareholders and investors. He prefers to own his companies. From Amber Day onwards, apart from his two bids for Marks and Spencer, Green mainly steered clear of public companies. Each business acquisition and subsequent sale made him money. From those deals he made the money to fund the next challenge and met the people who became important in his later business life. He was building up significant cash and connections.

CONFIDENCE BUILDING

In 1999, Green really made people sit up and take notice when he bought the Sears Group, the fashion and shoes business, and sold it off in parts. He sold several of its high street chains (such as Miss Selfridge and Wallis) on to the Arcadia group. He came out of that deal with serious money and everyone in the fashion business, the City and the banks were wondering where he'd strike next. He was now seen as a real player and the demon of the deals. He seemed convinced that he could do no wrong and his confidence had grown.

It had built to such an extent that he settled his aspiring gaze on one of the biggest retailers in the UK – Marks and Spencer. Admittedly it was in the doldrums, but it was an audacious aspiration. The country's beloved Marks and Spencer was a public company and some of the board members had been holding the reins for a long time. Green refused to be ignored. Once again he re-fused to take no for an answer.

Money always was a big motivator for Green, but it seems that the chase and the deal play a big part in the thrill too.

While Marks and Spencer was strug-gling, and the shareholders were get-ting increasingly impatient with falling sales, Green was putting together the money for his bid from a mix of private investors and the banks, deter-mined to get his hands on the biggest fashion retailer on the high street. Marks and Spencer had to take him seriously and fight back. The battle turned into a dirty tricks campaign over share dealings: several papers printed stories about his wife's shares in Marks and Spencer, and although any accusations had no foundation, one of Green's bankers withdrew support and Green pulled out of the race. Green successfully sued the newspapers concerned.

TRANSFORMING BHS

But the man never gives up. It's one of his most significant traits. Green had acquired a reputation as a shrewd businessman with an uncanny knack of making money, who could spot an opportunity and see a way to make things work.

Storehouse owned Mothercare and British Homes Stores (Bhs), which wasn't doing well. Before he'd made his brazen bid for Marks and Spencer, it was the kind of chain Green liked to buy and turn around. The Storehouse management didn't know what to do with it. Green simply made his offer, gave the board a deadline and did the deal. Green is not afraid to take a risk, but it will be a calculated risk. He will have worked out just what will happen if the risk doesn't come off. He'll have measured the consequences of making a bad decision before he decides whether the risk is worth taking. If he hadn't been sure he could make Bhs work, he wouldn't have bought it.

He's used his skills with sourcing and negotiating to bring stock to customers at prices they're willing to pay.

Bhs was the perfect opportunity for Green to show his business acumen as a top retailer. It brought with it a very valuable property portfolio that he could sell if all else failed. So to the surprise of staff and business watchers alike, rather than turning the business into a viable one and selling it again as quickly as possible, Green kept Bhs.

Green is clearly passionate about business, pays great attention to detail and is a hands-on boss. He stalked the floors of his new acquisition, getting to know it and working out how to make changes, cut costs and increase sales. One of his pet hates is said to be too many garments on a rail, and he was spotted helping to stack shelves and moving displays late at night. He likes things done his way and done quickly, and, within a year, profits had picked up. Green was cock-a-hoop at the turnaround in fortunes. He'd been proved right. The chain could work and he'd seen how to do it when no one else had, or had even been interested in trying.

GREENING THE HIGH STREET

Bhs made Green a formidable high street figure but it wasn't to satisfy him. It wasn't long before he was looking for a new deal. He was worth £1 billion by this time, so he certainly didn't need the money. Money always was a big motivator for Green, but it seems that the chase and the deal play a big part in the thrill too.

There were all sorts of rumours about what he was planning to buy up next, but in the end he went for Arcadia, a publicly listed company with Stuart Rose, the current outgoing Chief Executive and Chairman of Marks and Spencer at the helm. Arcadia cost Green £900 million and made him one of the biggest forces on the high street. He had created the UK's biggest private retail company.

From various interviews and press reports, it's suggested that being a private company is important to Green, as it means he can get on and run the businesses 'his way' and make things happen without having the shareholders breathing down his neck. Technically Arcadia doesn't belong to Green himself but to his wife Tina. He transferred control of the company to her in 2004. In reality, though, Green himself is very much in charge.

ANOTHER BID

But even acquiring Arcadia doesn't appear to have stopped Green's restlessness. He made another bid for Marks and Spencer in 2004. Again it eluded him. It seems to be the big prize without which he won't be content. Only time will tell whether it will be a case of third time lucky or whether Green has finally put that ambition behind him.

In the meantime, Topshop has become the jewel in the Arcadia crown and made Green a household name, the friend of top models and the subject of glossy magazines and gossip columns. He has poured his enthusiasm, drive and ambition into growing his business. He's used his skills with sourcing and negotiating to bring stock to customers at prices they're willing to pay, and his hands-on attention to detail has made Topshop the chain of choice for millions of customers. The recession has tested his retailing expertise and at the time of writing he's come out of the downturn well. So is he really the UK's best retail entrepreneur as some claim? Whatever history decides, he's certainly one of the richest and a power to be reckoned with. Whatever happens next, he's likely to do it his way.

DO IT YOUR WAY

- **You'll succeed if you never take no for an answer** – people will be more likely to find ways to solve a problem.
- **Spot something in the deal that benefits each party** in the way that Green does when he's taking over a company, and the deal is more likely to succeed.
- **Stay focused and stick to what you know.** Don't be afraid to take risks with what you know. Green sticks to fashion and the longer he's been in the business the better he's understood it, which reduces or minimises the risks.
- **Learn to spot the opportunities that others don't and act quickly.** Green spots opportunities partly because he follows his gut instinct and partly because he's got an in-depth understanding of the fashion and trends in fashion, and a 'feel' for what people want.
- **Work hard, be hands-on and pay attention to the detail.** Green knows everything there is to know about his stores, ranges and lines; he demands changes, and checks they've been made. It's hard work but it pays off.
- **Every time a business fails you learn a lot.** Move on and take the lessons with you. Green learned valuable lessons early in his career about making businesses run more efficiently and they made him a fortune later in his career.

2

MAKE THE BUSINESS RUN AS EFFICIENTLY AS POSSIBLE

'Throughout my career, I've always thought there was a fundamental difference between being efficient and being a cost cutter.'[1]

Philip Green

G reen is always looking for ways to run his businesses more efficiently. Some call it cost cutting, but as Green's quote in the opening of this chapter shows, to him there's more to being efficient than just reducing costs. The first part of his career, as we've seen, focused on buying up and rescuing failing businesses that no one else was bidding to buy. He closed parts of the operation and split the rest up into viable packages to sell them on at a profit. Some of his critics have accused him of asset stripping, but Green and his supporters would argue that by understanding how and where to make efficiency savings he saved many a business from going under. Green has carried on that drive for efficiency right through his retailing career and it's one of the main reasons his current businesses have flourished.

ASSET STRIPPING

Asset stripping is the practice of buying up a failing company and selling off the parts of that company for a profit. There's a fine line here: Green would argue that he was acting to protect the future of the companies he was involved in. Many of the firms he bought were in administration before his intervention and, in most cases, no other buyers were forthcoming.

His enemies said he was just out to sell off anything he could make a quick profit on, without regard for the firm or its staff; his friends supported and championed him as the ultimate turnaround merchant who could spot potential in businesses where others couldn't and who had an uncanny knack of putting together viable new businesses. Certainly there are people who were in trouble before he came on the scene who have reason to be grateful for his intervention.

A QUICK 'IN AND OUT'

Because Green is a man to get a deal done quickly and was in and out in a flash, his detractors also doubted that he'd ever be anything more than a wheeler-dealer. Green may not have kept his early businesses afloat, but he did seem to know how to cater for the mass market and that meant keeping the costs down.

Green is always looking for ways to run his businesses more efficiently.

When he brought cheap jeans in from Hong Kong, direct from the manufacturers, he was able to supply retailers in the UK with cheaper jeans than they could get elsewhere. He was at one time the biggest supplier of jeans in the UK. When he brought designer label clothes in from Europe at knockdown prices, he made them accessible to people who couldn't afford the prices in London's exclusive boutiques. These were efficiency savings Green could apply to future businesses … like Bhs, which he bought in 2000, taking it from a public company into private ownership.

OPPORTUNITY KNOCKS

Bhs had been struggling for a long time. It had made a loss of £8.3 million in the six months to October 1999. Its owner, the Storehouse Group, which also owned Mothercare, put it up for sale but no one else wanted it. The grocery people Iceland and the owner of Poundstretcher had briefly flirted with the idea of buying the chain, but as Richard Hyman of Verdict, the retail consultants, told *The Independent* at the time: 'It was a flawed concept. The various parts always operated independently and the synergies were difficult to see.'[2]

The shareholders were fed up with the firm's performance and its management. Bhs had been plagued by management changes and takeover bids, was making little impact on the high street, and was underperforming for the amount of space and number of outlets it had. It was just the kind of business that Green had become renowned for taking over. And despite all its flaws, Green could see potential that others had failed to spot. Bhs wasn't doing well, but Green only ever takes calculated risks. He would have been satisfied that Bhs also had the advantages of having a large number of good properties in great sites on the high street.

His hands-on management style seems to have been the key to Green's initial success at Bhs.

Good properties and great high street sites don't in themselves guarantee huge numbers of customers. Just because a shop is in the kind of location that thousands of people have to walk past every day, it doesn't mean they'll go in. They have to be offered something so enticing that it makes them go in. Bhs was the fifth biggest retail chain, had 161 stores and just over 2% of the clothing market. Given its size, it should have accounted for a bigger slice of UK clothing sales. Customers were passing it by to shop elsewhere. It was failing to compete with the newer stores on the high street.

IN THE FIRING LINE

When Green bought the company, everyone expected him to split up the business and sell off the valuable bits for a whopping great profit. But what he had in mind was running a much tighter ship, cutting out the fat, getting the costs down and selling better quality products at prices that customers would be prepared to pay. In short, turning the firm around and running it in the long term.

His hands-on management style seems to have been the key to Green's initial success at Bhs. He went through every aspect of the business to look for ways of reducing outgoings. To turn Bhs around, Green's detractors had predicted that he'd squeeze cash out of the business, reduce the stock and take longer to pay suppliers.

TAKING STOCK

When Green arrived at Bhs, he seemed to understand instantly why the chain was performing badly: 'We had 10,000 little dresses – the sort of thing Pocahontas would wear. We couldn't sell any of them … It was stuff that wasn't good enough for floor mats.'[3] There are various reports suggesting that things at Bhs were even worse than Green had anticipated.

A lot of the lines on offer weren't what Bhs customers wanted to buy or weren't at a price they were prepared to pay. Green could have accepted the new lines already ordered for the next season and repeated the process: rails and shelves full of goods no one wanted; cash tied up in that stock; prices marked down at the end of the season; falling profits and a struggling company. Or he could change things.

By all accounts, 'hands-on' in Green's case seems to mean that he knows just about everything about every aspect of Bhs.

He had to start somewhere and he started by renegotiating orders and contracts, and getting some lines into the stores that customers did want to buy. He had form, having done it before, but not even Green could stop a tanker in its tracks. He couldn't turn all the lines in a department store the size of Bhs around in one season, but his energy and enthusiasm is boundless, his attention to detail meticulous, and he undoubtedly has an eye for what works and what doesn't.

Green knows what his customers will pay and what they will expect to get for that price.

Green took the line with suppliers that he could go ahead with the contract that had been signed but the goods wouldn't sell and so there would be no money for another order next year; or they could renegotiate, supply different goods that would sell and they might all live to fight another day. Green had been working at the lower end of the clothing market for most of his career so he was well qualified and a lot of the tricks he'd learnt were put into practice. He knew how to deal directly with manufacturers; he'd learned about negotiating deals, importing and product. Green's critics blame him for being ruthless, but if the situation at Bhs was as bad as reports suggest, there may well have been no other way for the business other than down that pan taking thousands of jobs with it.

Green was able to negotiate better deals with suppliers and dealt with manufacturers direct where he could. He had all the right connections. Green also looked for new manufacturers who could fulfil orders more quickly and allow him to get more fashionable lines into the stores more quickly. That way he could entice customers to buy up-to-the-minute fashions more often.

Green's dealings with suppliers were a big part of the efficiency savings, but it wasn't just the clothes suppliers who were under review. He looked over every last detail of his business. By all accounts, 'hands-on' in Green's case seems to mean that he knows just about everything about every aspect of Bhs. He knows every garment in his stores including how much it cost to produce, what price it's on sale at, how many were bought in and how many have sold. He knows what it costs to display them and what it costs to run his properties and cars. He knows how much the gas and electricity costs. He knows how much staffing costs. Because of his attention to detail, he can work out how to keep down all those costs. That may be cost cutting, but it all adds up to efficiency.

THE PRICE IS RIGHT

Green's favourite part of the whole selling process is the merchandise. With his obsessive attention to detail he wants the best colours, fabric, design, cut and manufacture he can get for the right price. But along with that there's another skill that serves Green well, and this is where he reigns supreme according to my retail analyst: 'I believe his special skill is in knowing the absolutely right price for the product and getting it absolutely right first time.'

People who know how Green operates say he's the best at what he does, which is buying as cheaply as possible to sell for as much as possible with a healthy margin. Green knows what his customers will pay and what they will expect to get for that price. He has a real instinct for the right price for a particular product.

He then works backwards. If he wants to sell something at £10, he works out what he'll have to get the supplier to supply it for so that he can sell it at £10. So the negotiation with the suppliers is all-important. When he gets it absolutely right he doesn't end up with masses of little dresses unsold and marked down to half price, which is very important for the health of the business's cash flow. My retail analyst says that managing the cash is always Green's top priority:

> 'So long as you are efficient with the cash, everything else can come good. For example, when he acquired What Everyone Wants, he changed the original management's tack of slashing the price if sales were too slow and cut right back on the mark-downs. This hits volumes of sales, of course – which reduces market share – but it does wonders for margins.'

REDUCING BUREAUCRACY

Another aspect of the business Green was looking at was the staff. Bhs had been run as a public company and there were layers of management there he simply didn't need. By stripping those out, Green made more savings, had a closer relationship with his remaining managers and created a more efficient team.

Green has the kind of mind that can carry massive amounts of detail about his business. He can recall the cost of items and the prices they're sold at, how many were bought and how quickly they sold. He doesn't need members of staff to tell him those details or about the finances and the property, the sourcing and the buying. Because he has that kind of mind and is a hands-on manager who gets very involved in the running of the company, he needs fewer people to help him run it than most.

When there's a board and shareholders to answer to, decisions go through several layers. Green took out the layers and gave senior managers more responsibility. With fewer layers of management, decisions could be made much more quickly, as could the process of turning the stock around, redesigning displays and reducing prices on poorer selling lines, for example.

IT FIGURES

Green's attention to detail is what allows him to be so efficient, and it paid off. By the end of the first year profits were well up; by the end of the second year they'd trebled and all the loans had been paid off. By announcing the profits, Green came in for a lot of stick. Bhs was a private company so he didn't have to make the figures public. When the figures were scrutinized, according to Richard Fletcher at *The Daily Telegraph*, contrary to critics' expectations the number of stock lines had increased, suppliers had had to wait about three days longer for payment and 'the vast majority of growth has been delivered by increased profitability and increased sales.'[4]

> **'His turnaround at Bhs is a classic case-study in the merits of private ownership.'[5]**

Green had bought Bhs for £200 million in 2000 and the critics started to argue that he had got it too cheaply. But anything is only worth what someone will pay for it and he was the only buyer. Jeff Randall commented, 'His turnaround at Bhs is a classic case-study in the merits of private ownership. He regards all 160 stores as his own (they are) and is obsessive about every one.'[5]

The rise in the company's value bolstered Green's personal wealth. In 2002 he was estimated to be worth £1.2 billion because Bhs was worth five times what he'd paid for it.

Because Bhs is a private company owned by Green, he could make decisions more quickly than his rivals. But luck also played a part in the spectacular turnarounds of the Bhs fortunes. C&A, one of the main rivals to Bhs on the high street, closed its UK branches – and to some extent, Bhs filled the gap.

LANDING A BIG ONE

When Green bought Arcadia, he took it from public company into private ownership. The expected cull of staff there didn't happen, although Green did again trim down the upper layers of management – stripping out management layers and middlemen cuts costs dramatically.

But with somewhere in the region of 40,000 staff in his newly enlarged empire, Green had to rely even more on designers and buyers, and brand directors at the Arcadia chains kept their jobs and were given more autonomy. He set them targets, promised bonuses and helped them sort out their problems. Jane Shepherdson, the brand Director at Topshop, was one of those who benefited most and her brand flourished as a result. However, he still had the final say over many of the ranges.

Not only did fewer layers of management add up to reduced costs, but it led to a more efficiently run team.

He also stripped down the management structure, as he had done at Bhs. The managers who remained got quick responses from Green. He wanted up-to-date fashion into his stores at top speed. His customers saw things in magazines that they wanted to buy that day, not three months hence, and he wanted that fast turnover. He wanted to beat his rivals and set trends. It all required quick responses from the boss – something Stuart Rose, who had been Chief Executive of Arcadia before Green bought it, with a board to answer to, hadn't been able to do as effectively. Not only did fewer layers of management add up to reduced costs, but it led to a more efficiently run team.

As at Bhs, Green kept his eye on the detail of the running of the business and at ways of cutting costs. Increased profits came from a combination of cutting costs and attracting more customers, keeping them loyal with fast-moving new ranges and enticing them to spend more often.

UPS AND DOWNS

Despite Green's major efficiency drives at both Bhs and Arcadia, not everything ran smoothly.

Green proved himself as a retailer when he bought Bhs and Arcadia, and he proved that efficiency does indeed rule. He has the kind of mind that carries massive amounts of detail about his business and his stock. That allows him to do by himself what many other business people need several staff to help them do. His knowledge of the supply chain, experience of sourcing and his negotiating skills allowed him to build a business that's efficient without affecting the quality of his products. Simply cutting the costs of supplies can mean reduced quality or longer waiting times, which can jeopardise the retailer's relationship with the customers.

Cost cutting may lead to temporarily increased profits, but it can ultimately lead to lost customers. Efficiency is about reducing costs without the product or the customer suffering. Green achieves his efficiency by keeping a close eye on detail across his stores. However, he has also proved that if you are a person who does a lot of the jobs yourself and you take your eye off the ball, your efficiency savings can slip.

While he was immersed in his second attempt to buy Marks and Spencer in 2004, sales at Bhs slipped back. Green's skills in sourcing and efficiency could have benefited Marks and Spencer at a time when they were struggling, but while his attention was diverted from Bhs, profits there slipped and the firm has been bumping along ever since. In 2005, Green warned that profits would be down by a third and in 2006 profits halved. As he told *The Guardian*, 'you name it, we got it wrong – we had the wrong fashions, wrong shapes, wrong sizes'.[6]

Efficiency is about reducing costs without the product or the customer suffering.

Arcadia fared better than Bhs and profits are up 13% in the 12 months to September 2009. Green has been paying close attention to the Arcadia brands; Topshop, Topman and Miss Selfridge have been doing particularly well, proving again that for him keeping an eye on the detail pays off. Analysts think that his move in 2009 to merge Bhs with Arcadia will lead to further efficiency savings across the whole group. Ian Grabiner, who is now Chief Executive of the enlarged Arcadia, is a vastly experienced retailer who has worked for Green on and off for 20 years. He too is reported to be a man who is always on the lookout for efficiency savings and he's credited with many of the efficiency drives that have served Arcadia so well.

MAKE THE BUSINESS RUN AS EFFICIENTLY AS POSSIBLE

- **Don't let costs rise when profits are high.** The firms that do best are the ones with the most efficiently run operations. Keep a grip on costs. Green has always negotiated with his suppliers to keep costs down.
- **Know your products and the processes by which they get onto your shelves.** It will make it that much easier to see how to reduce the costs of getting them there. For Green it's not just about keeping the costs of his products down, but about keeping the costs of running the business in check too.
- **Cut out the middle wholesalers and suppliers.** This can reduce costs if you know how to negotiate those deals yourself. Green is a skilled negotiator and uses those skills to his benefit.
- **Reduce the layers of management.** This will help to cut costs if you know how to do those jobs yourself, and decisions can be made more quickly. Green doesn't need staff to help him with the finances or sourcing.
- **It's all in the detail.** Look at every aspect of the business to see where you could run it more efficiently … everything from the staff and suppliers to the fabric and zips; the hangers and rails; the gas and electricity bills. Green sees ways to save on every aspect of the business.
- **Manage the cash and get the prices right.** Green is brilliant at knowing what price the customer is willing to pay and keeps a tight rein on any cash due.
- **But be focused.** You can't afford to take your eye off the ball. Even Green has found that profits can slip if you're not paying attention.

3

KEEP THE CUSTOMER SATISFIED

'The thing with Philip is you know exactly where he's going … He loves the products, he's got passion and that permeates out to others.'[1]

Romney Drury, Marketing Director, Bhs

Green currently has eight different chains in his Arcadia Group. But why is it that at one end of the scale he has the very successful Topshop and Topman, while at the other there is Bhs, which does not seem to perform as well? My retail analyst suggests a possible reason:

> *'It all comes down to Talent. Topshop – and don't forget Topman, which has outperformed its sister chain at times recently – attracts top talent because of its cool prestige amongst fashionistas. The other, far less sexy chains, lack such automatic pulling power.'*

Green and his 'top talent' get it right because they know what will keep the customers satisfied. They may not get it absolutely right all the time for every customer, but the sales figures and profits would suggest that they're right more often than not.

Topshop is world famous and expanding; Topman often outperforms its big sister and little sister Miss Selfridge is doing well. Dorothy Perkins is attracting customers with the kind of products that get increasing publicity in the glossy magazines; Green has brought model Yasmin Le Bon and singer Beth Ditto on board at Wallis and Evans to give the brands a touch of the Kate Moss celebrity chic; and even Bhs is being revamped as it's merged into the Arcadia Group. Throughout the whole group there's an understanding that you have to keep the customer satisfied or they go elsewhere. But it's at Topshop that Green has set the customer service standard for the rest of the brands to aspire to.

Green and his 'top talent' get it right because they know what will keep the customers satisfied.

TOPSHOP TAKES OFF

Over the last few years, while the economy was booming, the high street was buzzing and chains were launching and expanding on the expectation of ever-increasing customer numbers. But one name was rising relentlessly to the top of the pile. With Topshop, and its little brother Topman, Green really does seem to know what his customers want and is giving it to them.

Topshop was founded in 1964 in the Peter Robinson department store in the north of England. A year later, Peter Robinson in London's Oxford Circus gave Topshop space in its basement. When Topman was launched in 1978 and then combined with the Oxford Circus Topshop in 1992, it became the world's largest fashion store. But the term 'fashion store' was an oxymoron until relatively recently as far as shoppers were concerned. It was considered to be deeply unfashionable and uninspiring in the 1980s and into the 1990s – analysts remember it as selling bland, ill-fitting, badly cut T-shirts to teenagers. But things changed in 1996 when *Vogue* magazine voted the chain's Colour Cosmetics the best new range on the high street. Glossy magazines have a lot of power over shoppers and the brand was helped on its way to becoming what it is today.

Style magazine *The Face* once called Topshop 'a dream factory that initiates and innovates, and creates its own fashion'.

Two years later the Oxford Circus branch was refurbished and reopened as the flagship store, and around 100,000 shoppers descended on it every week. The launch of a special 'Design Collection' helped to cement the brand's fashion credibility. And all of that was long before Philip Green set his sights on owning Topshop's parent Arcadia.

REACHING DIZZY HEIGHTS

Since then, Topshop's appeal has moved on from being a down-market teenage clothes shop to what is now – to the loyal customers I've spoken to – a seriously cool, sexy, headline-grabbing, trendsetting brand. Analysts hail it as the retail phenomenon of the high street and it's had the sales growth to back it up. It continues to make headlines in fashion magazines and the fashion pages of newspapers, and has a reputation for bringing innovation and style to the high street.

Topshop frequently sets the trends with hundreds of new ranges coming into the flagship store every week. Style magazine *The Face* once called Topshop 'a dream factory that initiates and innovates, and creates its own fashion'. This isn't a fashion chain dependent on clothes bought by an in-store buyer from a wholesaler who has already bought existing designs from a manufacturer. This is a chain that works out what its customers will want. Jane Shepherdson, the former Brand Director, gets much of the credit for having created this ethos before Green took over Arcadia. Green spotted her talent, allowed her the freedom to develop her ideas further and added his own talents to making Topshop a star. Topshop has its own designers to design the ranges, has them made up in selected fabrics and makes them so attractive that its customers 'must have' them.

Green may claim not to have the fashion eye, but he has the dealing and buying skills to know what the customer wants.

It has become one of the best-known UK fashion brands and opened a flagship store on Broadway in New York in 2009. Topshop now has more than 300 stores in the UK and around 100 in many more countries, reaching as far as Tokyo, Saudi Arabia and Los Angeles. They don't all have the pizzazz of the flagship stores, but the reputation and brand appeal is such that even if customers in the further reaches of the globe can't get the latest designer ranges, and have to make do with smaller stores and less choice, they stay loyal and a trip to Oxford Circus is top priority if they ever get to London. And there's always the chain's website for online shopping.

Think about the marketing and PR of the Arcadia Group's brands and it becomes apparent that Topshop has a much higher profile than the rest. It seems as if most of the money spent on marketing Arcadia brands goes on Topshop. It's all helped it to achieve cult status.

THE TALENT BEHIND THE TRANSFORMATION

Jane Shepherdson worked hard to change the down-at-heel store into the high street award winner it is today. She's no longer at Topshop, but started her career with the company and worked her way up from the stock room to assistant buyer and buyer. Her break came when she stuck her neck out and ordered tank tops – and sold half a million in a week. That move established her reputation for spotting trends and giving the customers what they want. Topshop has become a store with a distinctive personality. It's shopping as entertainment with all the glitz and razzamatazz of the theatre. In 2008, I was told by Jane Shepherdson that she got the ball rolling by putting into the stores the kind of clothes she and her buyers wanted to wear but had to go elsewhere to buy.

When Green bought Arcadia he kept Jane Shepherdson on and supported her ideas and decisions, and helped out if there was a problem. He has suggested that while he's a great retailer with an instinct or feel for what women want to wear, he doesn't know what will be on trend in that particular Topshop market. Luckily for him, Jane Shepherdson did. In November 2003 she was named as the most influential person in high street fashion by *Drapers* magazine, with her then boss in the number two spot. Admiring analysts say she follows her gut instincts to introduce elements that she feels are right for the brand.

Thirty-six-hour shopathons, free massages, nail bars, on-the-spot alterations, breakfasts and makeovers, personal shoppers, VIP sections, and designer ranges have all made Topshop top of the shops. What you get in the flagship stores is a real experience; shopping as entertainment. The shop is no longer just another stop on the high street but a destination in itself. People go to London to shop in Topshop and take in a few other stores while they're there.

FAST AND FRENETIC

Green is hands-on at Arcadia as he was at Bhs when he arrived. Reports abound of him adjusting window displays and keeping on top of the detail. He claims not to get involved in the design side of things and to leave that to his designers, but he does know about trends. In *The Independent* he recalls an incident in LA: 'I go to "shop the stores" ... This was Easter, April time. And the only thing they were selling were ponchos. Woollen ponchos in 90 degrees! ... I bought six of them and I DHL'd them back here. I said: "Get into this!" ... Wallis were first. And off we went! Ponchos were massive.'[2]

Perhaps the biggest draw is the fast-changing fashion. Around 7000 lines come and go every season at Topshop. Nothing hangs around on the rails for too long. The suppliers get the lines into the stores in double quick time and there's always something new; something that the customer simply must have. Green understands the draw of quickly changing lines: even customers who have no intention of buying just want to see what's new.

What Green brought to the Arcadia Group and to Topshop in particular were his buying skills. He knew how to get things from the manufacturers direct and get them into the shops more quickly. Customers were seeing celebrities in the papers and magazines wearing the things they wanted to buy, and so they had to be in the stores quickly or they'd shop elsewhere.

A key factor in Topshop's success has been the concept of shopping as entertainment.

Green may claim not to have the fashion eye, but he has the dealing and buying skills to know what the customer wants. Where Topshop was struggling to keep up with the newer chains like Zara, Green knew how to match them. The prices aren't the cheapest on the high street (they're more mid-market) – but if the clothes are special enough, customers are prepared to pay those prices. If there are new lines in the shops in weeks instead of a new collection every six months, you can drop in over and over again and you won't see the same clothes in the stores for months on end, becoming more crumpled and less appealing as the months drag by. If there's always something new and fresh, the temptation will be to indulge in a purchase. Getting that right is the mark of a good retailer.

Because the brand is credible in the eyes of customers now, people mix their designer tops with Topshop jeans or vice versa. They wear vintage with new. The brand has earned its own place in the wardrobes of UK shoppers and many of those are people who would never previously have crossed the threshold of anything other than designer shops.

THE EXPERIENCE

A key factor in Topshop's success has been the concept of shopping as entertainment. Go into the Oxford Circus store and you find clothes and shoes, but also the wall, the cafe, Boutique and Vintage. There are in-store events, such as seasonal catwalk shows, celebrity shoppers and makeovers. Visitors to the store spend, on average, almost three-quarters of an hour there.

I've asked dozens of analysts and retailers what they think is right about Topshop and the response was almost universal: the customers are getting something special, something they feel they really 'must have', at a price they're prepared to pay, in an environment they enjoy shopping in. It's retail theatre. It's not for everyone, of course, but then it's trying to attract the kind of shopper who enjoys the spectacle.

Unique, the chain's design label, was created in 2001 with the aim of setting the trends rather than following the catwalk fashion shows. Having a quick turnover of lines really helps achieve that result. There's Boutique – a specific area for more designer-conscious customers. The Topshop website is hugely successful too. There are style advisers, Topshop Sweets, Moto Sno-performance board and ski wear, lingerie, a one-hour delivery service by Vespa scooter, and of course the well-documented celebrity designers.

Topshop supports young fashion talent and has sponsored Graduate Fashion Week. It aims to launch the careers of young fashion students, supports London Fashion Week and sponsors the New Generation Award, which has been won by the likes of Alexander McQueen and Matthew Williamson. TS Design provides financial support to young designers by sponsoring their shows. In return, the designers put together a 'capsule' design collection for the in-house label. Topshop has gained a reputation for working with up and coming young talent, which not only helps create the next generation of style gurus but adds credibility and good PR for the brand.

CELEBS

Perhaps the one person who has done most to put Topshop on the map, or in the papers, is the supermodel Kate Moss and her designs for the chain. Polly Vernon of *The Observer* said after an interview with Green in February 2007: 'It sometimes seems as if every woman in the 17–47 age bracket is consumed by their exhaustive efforts to channel Moss chic. Green realized he could offer people the tools to do that more effectively.'[3]

Whatever people think of the clothes themselves, Kate Moss has delivered in terms of column inches and photo opportunities for the Topshop brand. Kate's ranges have been a huge success and have been followed by Stella Vine, Christopher Kane and Celia Birtwell, among others. It's a concept that Green is rolling out to other Arcadia chains with Beth Ditto and Yasmin Le Bon, and he has the pulling power to get the celebs to play ball.

GETTING IT RIGHT

When Green bought Arcadia (including Topshop) it became a private company, which allowed him to make fast decisions without interference from board and shareholders. He understood the draw of fast fashion and how to get it. He knew talent when he saw it and let Jane Shepherdson grow Topshop into the phenomenal high street leader it is today.

There were analysts who thought that Topshop's star would wane when Shepherdson left in 2007, but two years on, having experienced 18 months of one of the worst recessions to hit the street, it appears undimmed. Green understands that good talented staff are vital to keeping customers satisfied. He has a feel for what the customer wants and an instinct for what they will be prepared to pay for it. He knows how to source product at a price that will allow him to make a profits and he knows that the faster he turns around lines in his stores, the more often customers will be tempted to buy. To crown it all, he can attract the big names to work with him to give his business an attractive sparkle.

And he has another key skill – getting his businesses talked about. Even if he never adds up how much cash Kate Moss's designer ranges put in his tills, he'll know that the headlines and PR generated by her appointment and continuing association with Topshop were practically priceless.

Although Green has made Topshop a real winner as far as most of its customers are concerned, there has been one fly in the ointment. Green has had several run-ins with ethical campaigners, who accuse him of buying goods made overseas in sweatshops with unacceptable working conditions. There have been peaceful protests outside Topshop branches. He claims to check out all his sources to make sure working conditions are acceptable. But young shoppers – his target market – have become increasingly ethically and environmentally aware, and Green has introduced ethical clothing concessions and organic cotton in some brands.

HAPPY SHOPPERS

Topshop's loyal customers get what they want from the store. They get more than just the products; they get an experience they appreciate, too. But if you tried to emulate the Topshop experience in other stores, you may water down the appeal to the Topshop customers and you could annoy the customers who want a rather more sedate experience in less frenetic surroundings.

He understood the draw of fast fashion and how to get it.

Green seems to be picking out little bits of Topshop glitz and trying them in other stores to give the customers of each of the different chains what they want, such as great accessories at Dorothy Perkins, which are regularly photographed for the fashion magazines, and good collections at Wallis. And as he moves his Arcadia brands into his bigger 'brand houses' – some of them Bhs buildings – some of the stardust may well rub off on Bhs. There's more to be done if Green wants the rest of the chains operating at the level of Topshop and attracting the same volume of customers. But as far as Topshop is concerned it's working and it's a winner, keeping millions of customers very satisfied.

KEEP THE CUSTOMER SATISFIED

- **Work out what your customers want and give it to them.** Green always has his eye on what's selling and what's not.
- **Give them something special.** Keep the lines changing so that they 'must have' more, more often, and the sales will soar. Green is the master of getting new lines into his stores in the shortest possible time.
- **Watch, look and listen.** See how other people do things and you'll spot the trends. 'Shop the shops', as Green calls it; wherever he goes, he checks out what's selling, asks what's in demand, spots the trends and stays ahead of the competition.
- **Add a whole shopping experience.** Give a chain a distinctive personality and customers will love the brand. Green has made Topshop a globally famous brand.
- **Make customers feel special.** It breeds loyalty. Green loves the merchandise but knows it's the service that is the icing on the cake.
- **Spot talent and nurture it.** Support up-and-coming designers and your shop reaps the benefits. Green has built up Topshop with the help of great talent and now great talent comes to him.
- **Use the press to your advantage.** Glamorous headlines and photo calls are worth their weight in gold in advertising and PR terms. Every time Green appears in the press, his business gets free advertising.

4
WHATEVER YOU DO, DON'T BREAK THE SUPPLY CHAIN

'Green believes in the survival of the fittest approach!'[1]

Business analyst

You can't keep your customers satisfied if the supply chain breaks. Customers know what they want and if they don't find it in your stores, they go elsewhere. The Topshop experience shows that success lies with knowing what the customer wants, finding affordable manufacturers and suppliers who can help get the products out quickly, and letting your potential customers know it's there at a price they're prepared to pay for it. But if any link in that chain goes down, you have a problem. To that end, Green sees the supply chain as all-important.

LINKED IN

As a retailer, Green understands the need to keep manufacturers, other suppliers (where he uses them) and customers loyal and satisfied. It's a juggling act, but deals work best if there's something in them for all parties concerned. Green learned this from his own time with the wholesaler of shoes and as a supplier of jeans.

The Topshop experience shows that success lies with knowing what the customer wants.

As we've seen at both Bhs and Arcadia, Green found ways of cutting costs that inevitably allowed him to provide goods at cheaper prices. He cut costs by renegotiating existing contracts with suppliers or manufacturers, and cutting out middle suppliers and wholesalers altogether, where he could negotiate direct with manufacturers. It speeded up the whole 'design to customers' process.

If you accurately work out how much the customer will pay, negotiate a good deal with the manufacturer or supplier, and you don't have to pass all of those savings on to the customers, your margins and profits are greater. After all, that's what business is about – making money.

By working directly with manufacturers, you get your own designs into your stores, rather than being at the mercy of the 'eye' and instinct of a supplier or wholesaler. However, you can't have an eye for everything, and where Green has an eye for women's clothes in particular he also understands the value of good suppliers who know more about particular lines, and their sourcing, than he does. He does use middle suppliers, but as always he's looking to cut his costs and improve his margins.

There's no doubt that everywhere he goes he's thinking about what's coming up and what the customers will want to buy.

Critics said that manufacturers and suppliers to Bhs and Arcadia were squeezed. In some cases, Green moved to new manufacturers who could supply what he needed more cheaply. It is easy for big retailers with big buying power to change suppliers, because there will always be someone out there willing to take on the contract.

But there's a fine line to be walked. It isn't in a retailer's interests to squeeze important manufacturers and suppliers too tight. If a favoured manufacturer or supplier who understands your brand is put under too much pressure to cut their own margins, and goes out of business, you run the risk that you can't replace them quickly enough, and won't have the stock your customers have come to expect from your brand, and they desert you for pastures new. So was Green guilty of squeezing his manufacturers and suppliers? My retail analyst reckons so:

'... But no more than most successful traders. A key difference is his recognition of the partnership potential in his supplier relations. Middlemen have their uses, so he doesn't always seek to cut them out as one might expect. Some of his suppliers, like Richard Caring, have made as much money as he has.'

Green believes that you have to be open and honest with your suppliers, and they with you.

While Green claims not to be good at style, there's no doubt that everywhere he goes he's thinking about what's coming up and what the customers will want to buy. But even he needs trusted manufacturers and suppliers who can get the goods into his stores and trusted buyers and designers who do understand style. He did do a lot of the negotiations himself at Bhs, but he also brought in trusted old allies such as Richard Caring, a very experienced supplier who supplied most of the high street, to help review the ranges on sale. Caring has made his own multi-million pound fortune out of supplying retailers, so he too must have an 'eye' for trends and a feel for what retailers and customers want.

ALL IN IT TOGETHER

Despite what his critics think, Green seems to have a healthy regard for the supply chain. It's possible that there have been times when his manufacturers and suppliers have been squeezed, perhaps almost to the bone. There are certainly suppliers who no longer work with Green's businesses and were readily replaced. But his years of experience, and of trading through economically uncertain times, have underlined the importance of keeping the supply chain intact. Retailers need to have a relationship with their suppliers. In an *FHM* article of his top rules for career success, Green mentioned: '… suppliers never tried to take liberties with me because of my age. I realized back then that life's about fostering strong relationships.'[2]

When costs are rising and times are hard, retailers understandably don't want to pass on those rising costs to their customers in the form of price rises. The only way to avoid that is for the retailer to reduce their own margins or to demand that the supplier shares the pain. At some point, though, one or other – or both – run out of margin to cut. If valued suppliers walk away from deals with retailers because they can't make money, or go under, the retailers risk being left high and dry.

If one supplier can't cut the mustard, he'll find another who can.

Green believes that you have to be open and honest with your suppliers, and they with you. That doesn't mean everyone will always hear something they want to hear! Suppliers and manufacturers have to be able to come to the retailer for help. It has to be a partnership. If you have a distinctive brand, you need suppliers who understand that brand, and it can be damaging to your business to lose that relationship; and never more so than when the economy is doing badly. If a trusted manufacturer or supplier isn't paid by, or loses orders from, other companies, they could go out of business – leaving your orders unfulfilled.

Green has said that he wants his suppliers to come to see him so they can work through difficult times together. That's what my retail analyst means when he says that Green is different: because he recognizes the partnership potential in his supplier relations. Suppliers, however, say that the concept of partnership is lacking in retailing in general, and buyers are often unrealistic in their demands.

Despite his understanding of the importance of the supply chain and supply chain relationships, Green is still a tough businessman with his own business interests at heart. If one supplier can't cut the mustard, he'll find another who can. My business analyst says:

> 'Green deals on a global platform and if some suppliers go down, there will always be others willing and able to take the place of the fallen, as it offers them an excellent opportunity to get their goods to the public. In a speech a few years ago, I recall him commenting that it was the responsibility of suppliers to anticipate and prepare for requests for lower prices by constantly looking for ways to reduce their costs.'

SUPPLIERS' REVOLT

In 2006, the Arcadia Group was reported to have made itself very unpopular with its suppliers because it was extending its payment terms from 30 to 60 days. It was also demanding an additional 1% discount on all products from UK suppliers. Fashionunited.co.uk reported that Arcadia's Group Finance Director had suggested that the change was necessary if the brands were to keep their market share.

That was probably a realistic assessment, but the timing wasn't great. Green had awarded himself and his family a £1.2 billion dividend from the Arcadia Group in 2005, so it's not difficult to see why suppliers were disgruntled and many felt they were being asked to work for a much smaller return while he lined his pockets.

Almost before the ink was dry on the 2009 announcement that Bhs was to be merged into the Arcadia Group, angry suppliers were talking to the press. Lisa Berwin reported in a May 2009 issue of *Retail Week* that Bhs suppliers were being asked to bring their discounts into line with those of Arcadia – from 11.25% to 14.25%.

'Everybody has to tighten their belts all the way along the extended supply chain.'

Suppliers were furious and one criticized the timing of the move: 'They're bringing this in with only six weeks' notice and just after all the price negotiations for the Autumn/Winter ranges, and products have been negotiated.'[3]

However, not all suppliers disagreed with Green's methods or accepted that he was out of line. As another put it in an interview with *Retail Week*: 'Everybody has to tighten their belts all the way along the extended supply chain … We have to be critical in a constructive way and as a supplier we have to improve.'[4]

Green knows only too well that if you are offering your customers something special, your suppliers have to know your brand – and that means it's harder to find another supplier if one goes under. There's only so far they can be pushed. And in tougher times, retailers, suppliers, wholesalers and manufacturers are all in it together. The supply chain has to be kept intact.

WHATEVER YOU DO, DON'T BREAK THE SUPPLY CHAIN

- **Deal direct whenever you can.** Cut out the costs of the middle wholesalers and suppliers where you know your lines as Green does. He also knows when to keep his trusted wholesalers and suppliers where they know the products better.
- **Form an open and honest relationship with your suppliers.** It needs to be a two-way partnership. Green wants to know if trouble's brewing with a favourite supplier so he can take action to help.
- **Get the stock your customers want for the price they will pay.** If any one link in your supply chain, from manufacturers to customer, fails, your business can be at risk.
- **Find a manufacturer or supplier who understands your business.** It's well worth keeping them onside as Green does.
- **Get the best deal possible from your suppliers.** If you don't, you'll risk having to pass on rising costs to customers. That's where Green's negotiating skills come into their own.
- **Don't squeeze valued suppliers too hard.** Green can replace some suppliers with others who will supply him cheaper, but he knows that if a valued supplier goes under, his business could be badly affected.

5

PEOPLE MATTER – YOU CAN'T RUN AN EMPIRE WITHOUT THEM

'He has re-energized [Bhs'] people, its product and its way of operating, driving out bureaucracy and replacing it with a focus on the customer and product.'[1]

Amanda Hall, www.realbusiness.co.uk

Just as Green has a feel for what his customers want, he has an instinct about people. Like many entrepreneurs, Green tends to rely on his gut instinct rather than CVs when choosing staff. CVs aren't held in great regard by many entrepreneurs, partly because many of them may not have got anywhere if they'd been dependent on their CVs to get them work, and partly because most of them realize that the best people don't always have the best CVs.

Important staff at the top end of Green's business are usually headhunted and poached from other successful operations. They are also likely to be people Green has successfully worked with before or are 'talent spotted' and nurtured as they work their way up the inside. My business analyst says:

> 'He picks talent from competitors but he fires them quickly
> if it doesn't work out. The staff that he rates are very well
> paid with significant perks. For most senior staff, a vital
> requirement is that Green gets on with them.'

Green has a reputation for being demanding and difficult to work with, and there are former staff and suppliers who testify to having had a fraught working relationship with him. However, he has many staff who have stayed with him for a long time, or have left and returned, who find him a motivational boss. People who have skills that he doesn't have are respected and given the freedom to be their creative best. They seem to find his enthusiasm for the business invigorating and inspirational. Senior staff who have access to the boss get fast responses and the support they need from him to get on with the job.

'For most senior staff, a vital requirement is that Green gets on with them.'

There are many reports of Green shouting at staff and at suppliers when something isn't done the way he wants it, but most staff who have dealings with him point out that they learn to sharpen their skills. In any business there are staff and suppliers who find they can't work with the boss and have to end the working relationship, but in Green's case even people who have moved on accept that he's made businesses work where others might not have been able to.

BULLY BOY?

Green's reputation has come about to some extent because of disgruntled staff leaving his employment who have found him difficult and demanding, but reports in the press that suggest he has an abrasive nature and a tendency to use fairly ripe language when annoyed have probably added fuel to the fire.

People who have skills that he doesn't have are respected and given the freedom to be their creative best.

For all of the negative stories there are people who put his behaviour down to his meticulous attention to detail and demands for perfection. People who are as rigorous as Green about their businesses can often come across as ruthless and aggressive. Supporters say they wouldn't otherwise have got where they've got and their businesses wouldn't be so successful.

It probably makes a difference where members of staff are in the pecking order, and how much a boss needs them in the business, as to how they get treated. In Green's case there's probably elements of truth in all the points of views reported, but given the number of people who've worked with him for years, and those who go back to work with him again, the pros of working with someone with so many skills and so much knowledge and enthusiasm for the business must outweight any cons. My retail analyst agrees:

> 'He tends to keep people longer that his legendary "effing and blinding" would make likely. His genuine desire to be loved by the very people he's just insulted is another paradox.'

GREEN'S PEOPLE

Green has trusted people that he's worked with over the years. When it came to running Bhs and the Arcadia Group, he knew exactly who he wanted on his top team. Some of the people who were already on the staff when he took over the companies impressed him enough to be kept on: most of the brand managers stayed when he bought Arcadia, and Jane Shepherdson was the one who made the most headlines with Topshop.

Green has trusted people that he's worked with over the years.

Good buyers are important to Green. If they aren't buying the best possible stock at the right prices, customers will shop elsewhere. Unless you're prepared to buy every item you sell yourself, you have to find buyers who you think will translate your vision into goods – so where better to look than at other stores that are selling the kind of goods you want to sell? As a result, Green did employ some buyers from better-performing high street chains.

To keep on top of that side of things, Green brought in Richard Caring at Bhs to review the chain's various ranges with the buyers and made Elaine Gray his Chief Executive at MK One. He also employed his 'A' team – people who had agreed to work with him at Marks and Spencer had he been successful with his bid. They were big hitters like Allan Leighton who had turned around Asda and become Chairman, and Terry Green who'd done the same at Debenhams and become Chief Executive.

His friend the Scottish entrepreneur Tom Hunter, and the banker Robin Sunders, who'd helped him put his bid together for Bhs, came on board as non-executive directors. Between them the experience they brought to bear on Bhs was enormous.

As investors his bankers saw Green as a safe bet who would deliver them a good return on their investment.

IMPORTANT PEOPLE IN THE PHILIP GREEN STORY

Richard Caring is a good friend of Green's and advised him on products at Bhs. Caring understands product as a result of his own wealth of experience as a supplier. He and a girlfriend started out making mini-skirts on their own sewing machines and built up their business from there. He started importing knitwear into the UK from Hong Kong in the 1970s, set up International Clothing Designs and became the king of the Far East clothing industry. He cornered the market in quick turnaround fashion and when Green bought Arcadia he was supplying half of its clothes. He also supplied Bhs, Next, and Marks and Spencer. He now owns several top London restaurants such as The Ivy and much of his business on the clothing side is in the US. His experience in the Far East and in getting designs into the shops quickly was exactly what Green needed at Bhs.

Ian Grabiner, appointed Chief Executive of Arcadia in 2009, has been described as the 'engine room' of Green's empire and the key to its success. They first worked together when Green was running Amber Day; in 2002, Green brought Grabiner to Arcadia to replace Stuart Rose as Chief Operating Officer. Grabiner has kept a tight rein on costs and overheads and helped Arcadia to increase its profits during the recent recession. Like Green, he is focused on efficiency. Grabiner led the opening of Topshop's flagship New York store and the integration of Bhs into Arcadia. He's now Green's right hand man as Chief Executive of Arcadia. He's the numbers man and keeps a tight grip on operations. He's one of the colleagues Green has respected during his career and Grabiner seems happy to stay on at Arcadia, helping to keep it ahead of its competition.

Elaine Gray was buying director at What Everyone Wants when Green bought it for Amber Day. She left school at 16 and had worked her way up at the company, learning her buying skills there. Green always understood the value of good buyers and after working with her at Amber Day, he brought Gray in to work with him again at Owen Owen and then MK One. With Gray's help, Green overhauled MK One from a discount chain into a young fashion retailer. They also turned it from a loss-making business into a very profitable one and Gray eventually bought Green out. Green called on Gray again to help him sort out the buying and review the business at Bhs. Green trusted Gray and there are people in the retail business who say that Green learned much of what he knows about buying from Gray.

Sir Tom Hunter is the multi-millionaire Scottish entrepreneur. Green met him when Hunter supplied sportswear to What Everyone Wants. They both left school at 16 with few academic qualifications and have the ability to spot a business opportunity. Where Hunter can grow a business from scratch, Green is the dealmaker. While Hunter owned the Scottish firm Sports Division, Green negotiated a deal for him to buy the much bigger Olympus Sport from the Sears Group. The two have enjoyed a friendship and a business relationship ever since. Green taught Hunter a lot about doing deals and earned a multi-million pound share when Hunter sold Sport Division in 2000 to JJB Sports. In turn, Hunter has backed some of Green's ventures. He bought a small stake in Bhs when Green bought it in 2000 and was also on the board of Bhs.

Sir Stuart Rose was running Arcadia when Green bought the group and stayed on for a few months after Green's takeover. Like Green he has a reputation for being good at taking on and turning around struggling companies. He started as a management trainee with Marks and Spencer and worked for Burton, Argos, Booker and Arcadia. When he returned to a struggling Marks and Spencer as Chief Executive in 2004, Green was making his second bid to buy the company and it became a battle between Rose and Green. Green respects Rose's retailing skills and had approached him to run a Green-owned Marks and Spencer if his bid was successful. Although Rose could have run it with Green for much greater financial reward, he walked away from the offer. High-profile advertising campaigns with the likes of Twiggy, and a new commitment to the environment, helped sales and the Marks and Spencer share price recovered. By the end of 2007 the figures were looking rosier.

Jane Shepherdson, the Brand Director at Topshop when Green bought Arcadia, was credited with turning the brand into one of the most coveted labels on the high street. With Green's knowledge of sourcing and the supply chain, she produced fast-changing lines that were irresistible to customers who passed the door.

Having worked from the bottom upwards, when she reached buyer position at Topshop, she had a good idea of what customers wanted and a big say in what went on the rails. Green spotted her talent when he arrived at Arcadia and gave her more freedom to be creative with her brand and a helping hand when required. Green respected Shepherdson's feel for what Topshop's customers wanted and together they turned the chain from a place to shop into a shopping experience.

BANKERS

Not only can Green attract top retailers to work with him, but over the years he has been able to count on the support of a range of top bankers. Those relationships have been very important when it's come to putting deals together or making his bids for Marks and Spencer. When Green needs money and advice on his deals, like any other entrepreneur, he needs bankers, and as investors his bankers saw Green as a safe bet who would deliver them a good return on their investment. They recognized his ability to spot a business opportunity and make it profitable.

Green believes in paying bonuses where they're due, for a job well done and targets met.

Robin Saunders is an American banker with the German bank WestLB who helped finance the Bhs purchase and who had a stake in the company equivalent to just over 0.5%. Bob Wigley was a big name in investment banking. He was head of Merrill Lynch Europe until the beginning of 2009 and advised Green on his takeover of Arcadia and his 2004 bid for Marks and Spencer. Perhaps the best known of Green's influential banker friends is Peter Cummings. He joined the Bank of Scotland at 16 and worked his way up. By 2005 he was Head of Corporate Finance at HBOS and had become an admirer of Green's business methods, and helped him out with several of his deals.

Green impressed these people with his negotiating skills and his ability to turn around previously loss-making businesses and repay his debts quickly. The relationships were mutually beneficial. Green may have had to ditch some of his deals without the support of bankers and the various banks made significant amounts of money by investing in Green's deals. Peter Cummings, in particular, earned HBOS billions of pounds in the good times and some of that was made from his backing of Philip Green.

GATHERING MOSS

Green's association with the supermodel-turned-clothes designer Kate Moss is the one that sealed his celebrity status. It all started when Green won the bidding for a kiss with Moss at a charity auction. He allowed Jemima Khan the honour and the papers had a field day as Moss and Khan played to the cameras with a long smooch. A fortnight later, Moss and Green bumped into each other in a restaurant and she reportedly said, 'I'm a girl from Croydon; you're a boy from Croydon; why don't we do something together?' It's one of those quotes that's appeared in the press so often it's either true or it's better than the original, and no one has seen fit to deny it.

Whatever the truth behind his reputation, young talent wants to work at Topshop and Topman for the experience and the kudos.

What she had in mind was a range of clothes for Topshop. Green gave her his private number and left. Kate phoned and, less than a year later, the deal was done. When Green announced that Topshop was to launch a collection by Kate Moss the press went crazy. Green told the *Daily Mail* that Moss was 'smart and witty, and the six designers, buyers and merchandisers I assigned to work with her found her ideas totally inspiring'.[2]

GUT INSTINCTS

Whether its staff or bankers, investors or supermodels, Green prides himself on his gut instincts – although they haven't always been as sharp as he'd have liked – as the Amber Day events showed. He's been criticized for putting profits and dividends before his businesses and staff, but none of it seems to have done any real damage to his reputation.

The paradox is that Green is perceived as someone who does a bit of shouting as part of the act, but who really wants to be loved and admired for his prowess as a retailer. However, even Green knows that he can't run 12% of the UK's clothes shops if he can't attract and keep the right people. To that end, Green believes in paying bonuses where they're due, for a job well done and targets met. He's said to pay slightly over the odds in his stores. Retail is a highly competitive sector, not just in the selling of goods but in the recruitment and retention of good staff. Green knows from experience that at the top of the management chain it can be next to impossible to find the right people. It's taken him years to appoint a Chief Executive for Bhs and he's only achieved that by appointing the brilliant Ian Grabiner over the whole of the Arcadia Group. So it's vital to hold on to you best staff.

Green may pay over the odds and believe in bonuses to buy the loyalty of staff that he knows he needs to keep. Or he may be realistic enough to know that he can't afford to lose good staff to the competition. Many have been nurtured as they've moved up through his businesses and they've learned from his innovative, imaginative, risk-taking way of doing business. He wouldn't want to lose that investment or know-how. Inevitably, the staff who've left his employment are the ones who've described him as someone who makes all the decisions, and the ones who've stayed who claim he's an inspiration to work with. Whatever the truth behind his reputation, young talent wants to work at Topshop and Topman for the experience and the kudos – and older talent seems to stay or keep coming back.

PEOPLE MATTER – YOU CAN'T RUN AN EMPIRE WITHOUT THEM

- **Find the right people.** You can't run a huge empire like Green's or even a small business without them. Green looks for them in colleagues he's worked with in the past and nurtures those on his own staff.
- **Look beyond the CV.** Often the right people don't have the best qualifications – look beyond that at what they can do that you need for your organization. You need people who have the skills that you lack. Green looks at what people can do rather than what it says on a piece of paper.
- **Make sure they want to stay.** It's expensive to recruit and train staff – so take care of them, and remember that money isn't the only incentive. Green does pay slightly more than the going rate and offers bonuses, but he also gives his talented people freedom to flourish.
- **Show your passion for the business and the detail.** Staff want to be inspired and motivated by an inspirational, enthusiastic leader, but be careful that doesn't stray over into overbearing, ruthless behaviour!
- **Don't forget the rest of your empire.** It's not just your staff who are important to your business: advisers with relevant experience and board members who can guide you through different aspects of your business are a godsend. Green appoints trusted friends, former colleagues and bankers to his board.
- **Celebrity has pulling power.** Someone who can make headlines for your business is worth more than you could ever afford in advertising! Green understands the appeal of finding the right 'name' for each of his chains – someone the customers identify with.

6

SPOT THE MONEY-MAKING OPPORTUNITY

'Sir Philip Green is the unchallenged king of the British buyouts ... He is stocky, opinionated, fast talking and endowed with one of the best analytical brains in the business.'[1]

Robert Peston, author of *Who Runs Britain?*

Making money is one of Green's motivating factors and despite the odd setback he has progressed upwards in the financial listings. In 2009 he was at number six on the *Sunday Times Rich List*, up from ninth place in 2008.

As we've seen, by the time Green had been in business for 15 years – importing cheap jeans, buying designer label clothes from Europe and selling them in the UK at hugely discounted prices, trading at the lower end of the market – he had little to show for it financially. He had three companies in receivership at one time. But he'd learned some very valuable lessons and from 1979 onwards he earned himself a reputation for being able to spot opportunities with failing companies and finding innovative ways to keep them afloat – taking a share and building a small fortune in the process. Each time he moved on he made money.

DEAL OR NO DEAL

Green's deals over the years have been so numerous that it's impossible to go into detail. His rescue, turnaround and sale of Jean Jeanie to Lee Cooper, mentioned earlier in this book, was seen as one of the business successes of the 1980s.

The mid-1990s were full of money-making opportunities for Green and he seized many of them.

That was followed by his initially successful turnaround of Amber Day. But as we've seen, that came unstuck for several reasons which conspired to force his resignation. His supporters argued that he'd proved himself a retailing genius who could still make a profit in recession. For his part, the experience left Green determined never to run another public company. But he did walk away from the experience richer with a payoff and sold his shares in the company once the share price had rallied a bit. He was reported to have made more than £7 million.

Green was unstoppable – doing what he loved best – spotting opportunities, going for them and making money.

Perhaps it was a case of whatever doesn't kill us makes us stronger – but Green relaunched himself and has never really looked back since. The man has an awesome staying power and it wasn't long before his dented reputation had been repaired and almost forgotten.

ON A ROLL AND ROLLING IN THE CASH

The mid-1990s were full of money-making opportunities for Green and he seized many of them. In 1993 he bought the failing discount fashion firm Parker and Franks, and turned it into Xception. He then bought Owen Owen, the fifth largest department store chain in the UK, and sold eight of the thirteen stores two years later in 1996. The money from the sale cleared the company's debts.

He bought 'One Up' from Terence Conran's Storehouse and sold it on a few weeks later to Primark. Next came Owen and Robinson with its jewellery and footwear arms, for which he came up with a rescue plan. Then he negotiated Tom Hunter's buyout of Olympus Sports from Sears and made a tidy profit for himself when that later sold to JJB Sport. That was followed by Mark One, the discount fashion chain for teenagers. Green then bought 185 Shoe Express stores from the Sears Group, turning 75 of them into Mark One stores and selling the remaining 110 stores to Stead and Simpson for more than double what he'd paid for all 185 shops. Green was unstoppable – doing what he loved best – spotting opportunities, going for them and making money.

IT'S A BUZZ

The buzz of doing the deal, buying up the property and selling it on at a profit seems to have been his motivating factor throughout the mid-1990s. He was constantly on the lookout for the next deal. His critics suggested that it pointed to his inability to make things work in the long term, that he wouldn't succeed as a retailer and was in reality little more than the same old wheeler-dealer as in his early twenties.

'Sir Philip Green has a unique three trump card hand: he has an equally deep understanding of products, property and proceeds.'

Maybe that was true at that time, but he later proved his critics wrong and didn't let the constant sniping slow him down. If Green had settled down to make one chain work, he would have missed the other opportunities that came his way. Just as he's now focused on fashion retailing, back then he was focused on the deals.

What's interesting is that most of his acquisitions have been chains that no one else seemed to see much value in. Despite criticism that he was simply stripping the assets, many analysts say he was actually breathing fresh life into retailing at a time when, without him, other chains might well have simply gone out of business. He had to have an understanding of retail to see a way to make something work that no one else wanted to take on. Analysts credit him with playing a big part in revitalizing retailing on the high street in the 1990s.

MOVING ON

In 1998 Philip and Tina Green moved to Monaco to live. They said it was something she'd wanted to do for a long time and that they were concerned about Philip's health. His critics suggested the move might have more to do with the tax advantages of leaving the UK to live in the tax haven. Whatever the truth of the move, Green met the super-rich Barclay Brothers as a result of it and the stage was set for the next big deal ... Sears itself.

When he left Amber Day in 1992, he was worth around £9 million; ten years later Green was worth more than a billion.

Green had bought Olympus Sports from Sears for Tom Hunter, and Shoe Express from Sears for himself. Now he took the remainder of Sears with the help of the Barclays and the banks. The Sears' chains Freemans and Adams Childrenswear were sold and Arcadia – which already owned Topshop, Topman, Dorothy Perkins, Evans and Burton – bought Outlet, Miss Selfridge, Wallis and Warehouse. The whole deal made Green and his fellow investors £250 million in profit in just a few months. Some analysts saw it as a brilliant coup, others again saw it as an object lesson in asset stripping and money-making. My retail analyst says:

> 'His property prowess is phenomenal – just look at the Sears deal. It was a stunning result and a key element was his real estate partners. Sir Philip Green has a unique three

> *trump card hand: he has an equally deep understanding*
> *of products, property and proceeds, as good – if not better*
> *– than the best individual professionals in each of those*
> *domains.'*

Praise indeed, but whatever the analysts thought, perhaps more importantly the City loved him once more. But however brilliant the Sears deal had been, the next move was breathtaking!

BIDDING FOR THE TOP

When Marks and Spencer appeared to be struggling in 1999, Green decided to go for the top prize and make a bid for the company, putting together a multi-billion pound bid. His previous acquisitions looked like small fry in comparison but he succeeded in getting the backing for the money he needed.

In the end, one of his bankers pulled out and Green had to drop his bid. If he was wounded, it was only a wound to his pride. Big banks had been willing to lend him serious money. He had convinced significant players that he was a serious player, had the right plans for Marks and Spencer and could make it work. When he withdrew, the Marks and Spencer share price fell to a nine-year low. He may have been down but he certainly wasn't out.

A CONSOLATION PRIZE

A couple of months later he bought British Homes Stores (Bhs). Most of Green's fortune, which by then amounted to around £140 million, was tied up in his MK One stores. He put up £20 million of his own money for the bid and borrowed most of the rest.

Robin Saunders at WestLB, with whom he'd work on the Marks and Spencer bid, put the deal together, and she and Tom Hunter each put some of their own money into the venture. Some of the big names Green had persuaded to work with him if he managed to buy Marks and Spencer agreed to come on board if he was successful. And so Green bought Bhs for £200 million, buying out all the shareholders and taking the company into private ownership.

While Green is always trying to spot money-making opportunities he only looks for them in the industry he knows best.

The deal had been done quickly and the chain proved to be in worse condition than Green had realized. But then he'd taken a gamble with very little of his own money and knowing that the property could be sold off if necessary. As we've seen, within two years profits trebled to £100 million, Bhs was valued at £1 billion and Green was listed by the *Sunday Times* Rich List as the thirteenth richest person in the UK, worth around £1.2 billion. When he left Amber Day in 1992, he was worth around £9 million; ten years later Green was worth more than a billion. It has been written up as the fastest 'billion' in history.

BAGGING ANOTHER BIG BEAST

Arcadia was deep in debt at the end of the 1990s and although sales were fairly good, it had been struggling when Stuart Rose arrived to run it in November 2000. It owned Topshop, Topman, Miss Selfridge, Evans, Wallis, Dorothy Perkins and Burton, and Rose had sold off some of the less well-performing chains such as Principles – which has since disappeared from the high street, a victim of the recent recession.

Green wanted to take Arcadia into private ownership as he had Bhs. He decided to make a joint bid with the Baugar Group, Arcadia's biggest shareholder, but this ultimately fell flat when Green later found out that the Baugur Group was being investigated for financial fraud in Iceland.

Redoing his calculations, he worked out that he needed to find an extra £200 million to fund the takeover and turned to his old ally Peter Cummings. Arcadia accepted Green's offer; and so Topshop and its stable mates became owned by the Green family. It cost him around £900 million and he became the owner of the biggest private fashion retailer in the UK.

The extended Arcadia is now the UK's biggest private retail company and second only on the high street to Marks and Spencer. Two years after the takeover, in 2004, Green was listed as the UK's fourth-richest man and worth £3.6 billion.

THE £1.2 BILLION PAYOUT

In October 2005 the newspapers reported that Philip Green had awarded himself the biggest dividend cheque in the history of UK business. The money came from the Arcadia group and was four times the group's pre-tax profits of £253 million. Green owned 92% of Arcadia and his share was £1.17 billion, with HBOS – the bank – taking the rest.

The money was borrowed. The business could well afford it according to Green. It was to be paid back over seven and a half years, was easily affordable, and left plenty of room for growth. He also pointed out that it was much less than venture capitalists would have expected to take out of the business.

But the episode left a stale taste, with some staff feeling disappointed and vulnerable. Many felt that Green wasn't the committed, passionate, enthusiastic boss they'd thought but just out to make money. And because it was paid to Tina Green, who technically owns the company and lives in Monaco, the money wasn't taxed. That caused a massive furore, with critics accusing Green of plundering the company's coffers and analysts speculating that he was building up his own personal bank account to take another shot at Marks and Spencer.

The £1.2 billion payout actually wasn't as big as it seemed, because it included a £460m dividend Green had announced the previous year but didn't take. My retail analyst thinks that 'so long as he's generous with his employees, they're less likely to deprecate his own generosity with himself.'

He's looking for businesses that he can run more efficiently while giving the customers what they want.

2009 is reported to be the fourth year that Green hasn't paid himself dividends.

STICK TO WHAT YOU KNOW

While Green is always trying to spot money-making opportunities he only looks for them in the industry he knows best – fashion retailing. He hasn't ventured away from that. There were reports that he was thinking of bidding for both Safeway and Sainsbury's, and supermarkets would have been a significant change of direction for Green – but neither chain ended up in his shopping basket.

For Green, an opportunity is a business that he can buy at a good price and add value to, cheaply. Green's skills are what add that value. He's looking for businesses that he can run more efficiently while giving the customers what they want. That means better sourcing, negotiating more beneficial contracts, removing unnecessary layers of management and cutting operational costs. He has never let shortage of cash stop him. Someone will be enthusiastic about the venture and put money into it if you can show them you have the right plans for the firm you're buying. That's where Green's relationships with his bankers have been important – they are convinced that he can spot the opportunities and has the skills, so he can borrow. He borrows, pays the debts quickly and grows the business.

He's a master at spotting the chance, pulling it all together and getting the backing and buy-in of the key people.

Green has spotted scores of business opportunities in his career and has made billions from them. He has a real knack for it but he also acts quickly before other investors get interested. Of course he's had help along the way, as we've seen, from his family to get started, and from wealthy friends, and his important banking connections who've backed his hunches. But he's a master at spotting the chance, pulling it all together and getting the backing and buy-in of the key people. Without their trust in his abilities he couldn't do that and his passion, energy and enthusiasm for the business he knows inside out are infectious.

SPOT THE MONEY-MAKING OPPORTUNITY

- **Spot the opportunity and go for it before someone else beats you to it.** Green has the knack but he also sticks to the kind of business he knows best.
- **Cut out the fat and reduce costs.** Some of the best opportunities come from businesses that have been badly run by their management team. If you can turn a business around, you can make money.
- **Consider borrowing against property.** Property is a useful asset against which to borrow to finance your venture, but take care before you put your own home on the line. Green was borrowing against properties in the family investment business or belonging to his own businesses.
- **Borrow what you need.** If you have a network of wealthy friends and bankers who believe in your abilities and in your plans for the business – like Green – you can borrow what you need.
- **Never let shortage of cash stop you.** Green borrows, repays the debts as quickly as he can from profits and grows the business.
- **Pay yourself a good dividend.** If it's your own company, and it can afford it, you should reward yourself with a bonus as Green does in good years. But don't take out of the company money you really need to reinvest.

7

WHEN THE GOING GETS TOUGH – WORK HARDER!

'Business is going to be tough certainly for the next year, I don't see any easing in the next 12 months.'[1]

Philip Green

Green has been in the fashion business for around 40 years, so the 2008/9 recession wasn't the first time he'd traded through tough economic times. He'd made money when others found the going too tough and when other businesses were going bust. Costs go up in recessionary periods, but many customers lose their jobs or overtime, and find their income going down. It's no time to pass on higher costs to fewer customers in the form of price rises, so Green had to try to do more to keep his costs down and prices stable. All his efficient housekeeping stands him in good stead but it's always a time to work harder if only to stand still.

LEAN TIMES

Green has traded through lean times in the mid-1970s, at the beginning of the 1980s and the end of the 1980s into the early 1990s. We have had 15 years of almost constant growth since 1992, but even in that period there have been trading dips when shoppers retreated and sales dropped. Green has been in the fashion business throughout all those peaks and troughs.

All his efficient housekeeping stands him in good stead but it's always a time to work harder if just to stay still.

In the 1970s, Green bought the stock of several failed businesses cheaply and sold the designer clothes to appreciative shoppers at heavily discounted prices. He then went to Europe for more of the same. He found he could buy the previous year's designer ranges at a reasonable price and that he had a good market for them back in the UK. He made money while retailers with exclusive shops and high overheads were unable to.

In the late 1980s, Green made money at Amber Day with the discount chain What Everyone Wants when others were going out of business. Even when his profits forecast for Amber Day proved to be wildly overestimated, and he had to resign, his supporters pointed out that he was one of the few retailers who had made a profit in the recession.

What Green seems to have learned through his experience of the tougher times is that the more efficient the business, the better able you are to weather the economic downturns. By keeping his costs down and repaying debts quickly in the good times, Green's businesses were in good shape to sit out recession.

NEVER MIND THE PROFITS

As the 2008/9 recession kicked in, Green knew from experience that profits would be harder to come by but that they weren't a priority. He didn't need to grow his businesses, so he didn't need huge profits. He just needed to keep enough customers buying to keep the bills paid and he was convinced he had a solid enough customer base to hang on until the economy improved.

The retailers that disappeared from the high street had nothing special to offer, so cash-strapped or worried customers deserted them – leaving them struggling to meet loan repayments and cover their rents. With credit drying up, banks were unwilling or unable to lend to keep them afloat. Where Green could ride out the storm, others weren't so lucky or hadn't been so prudent in their household management. But he still had to keep the customers coming in and that would mean working harder to give them something special they just had to buy! He told the BBC: 'You have got to find your niche now more than ever … You can't kid the public; you have got to work a lot harder at delivering the right merchandise.'[2]

As we've seen, Green is the master of speed. Lines move in and out of his chains fast, giving customers reason to pop in often to see what's new. There's always something fresh so there's more incentive to buy, and his designer and celebrity ranges give them something special. The theatre of Topshop and the influence of Kate Moss has been all the more important throughout the recession.

In the late 1980s, Green made money at Amber Day … when others were going out of business.

Analysts predicted that shopping patterns would change; that middle-market shoppers would move to cheaper stores like Primark and New Look; that the people with money would stay at the upmarket end of the retail sector even if they did buy slightly fewer items and it would be the middle market that was worse hit. Some of Green's chains have been hit to a certain extent, but Topshop, Topman and Miss Selfridge seem to have been offering enough that's special to keep their customers. They've attracted more upmarket shoppers looking for something cheaper to mix with their designer labels in the way Kate Moss carries off so well. And the middle market hasn't been so badly hit as predicted. As interest rates have fallen to record lows and brought mortgage payments down, people who still have jobs have found themselves with more money to spend.

As the UK's economy ran into the buffers and the signs of strain reached the high street, most analysts and business journalists were agreed on one thing: if Philip Green's chains didn't make it through the tough times ahead, it was likely that no one would. Most agreed that he was the man who could make it. What a vote of confidence in the retailer who runs the biggest private retail group in the UK – and at the time of writing, Green seems in a fairly good position. As my business analyst puts it:

> 'His lean approach appears to have prepared his businesses better than most for the recession. That said there is evidence of his businesses being hit, but not in a highly significant way.'

IT'S OFF TO WORK WE GO

Green certainly seems to be of the 'when the going gets tough, the tough get going' school of business. He is tireless, with boundless energy and a new challenge just seems to renew his enthusiasm.

His approach to difficult times is not to throw in the towel but to work harder. In Green's case, working harder isn't just about spending more hours in the office or on the shop floor, making sure the ranges and lines are right. It's also about finding more ways to attract customers and to keep his businesses in the public eye.

As we've seen, one of Green's ten secrets to business success is to look for opportunities at all times, and when you spot them, move quickly to get in there before the competition. So even as Green was working harder at keeping his existing businesses doing well, he had his eyes open.

TO BUY OR NOT TO BUY?

Recession is a time to consolidate and sit tight until profits improve, but it's also a good time to snap up bargains. Green was the master of that in the 1970s and 1980s, and this time he's taken more than a passing glance at a few struggling businesses.

In October 2008 he mounted a rescue bid for several chains – including Oasis, Jane Norman and Warehouse, which were owned by the Icelandic investment company Baugur. As soon as word got around that Green was interested, other buyers materialized. If he hadn't made an approach the various brands may have disappeared from the high street, but now their future looks more secure.

'His lean approach appears to have prepared his businesses better than most for the recession.'

He then bought a 28% stake in Moss Bros, which he sold on for a reported £1.2 million profit. He may not have added to his stable, but he has taken a leading role in shaping the high street that emerges from this recession. Since then he has been reported as saying there's nothing around that he feels he could add value to. But is he still in the market for the right deal when it comes along? My business analyst, speaking in November 2009, thinks so:

> 'The critical mass of his business empire will ensure survival and his total cash flow and access to further funding will probably result in him buying assets of other less fortunate businesses during the next 18 months.'

CONSOLIDATION

In the meantime, consolidation has been the name of the game. Green hasn't taken his eye off Arcadia and Bhs. He's merged the two to cut overheads and improve efficiencies further. If they share buildings or back office functions like human resources and finance, he can reduce costs. Some of Arcadia's smaller stores have leases that are due to expire soon and, as smaller space is more expensive, there will be considerable cost savings in putting the various Arcadia brands into the bigger Bhs stores, where they exist in the same high street. There's no suggestion, however, that in a street with both a Topshop and a Bhs, the Topshop will reappear in the Bhs building. Green surely can't expect that the people who shop at Topshop would be seen going into a Bhs store, can he?

If he hadn't made an approach the various brands may have disappeared from the high street, but now their future looks more secure.

Some analysts say the move is long overdue and will lead to greater efficiencies and boost Arcadia profits considerably. The group will end up with fewer, bigger stores and some of the smaller shops that housed individual brands will close. My retail analyst says:

> 'Moving Arcadia brands into Bhs is good news for the latter, but it's bound to besmirch the cachet of the former. One can see the logic in theory, but it's all happened before in the 1980s when [retail entrepreneur Sir Ralph] Halpern tried to do the same with Arcadia and Debenhams. It didn't work then and Debenhams was a far classier fascia than Bhs, so why should it now?' (Arcadia and Debenhams demerged in 1998.)

Profits at Arcadia are up – his last reported figures showed an increase of 13% for the 12 months up to the end of September 2009. Topshop, Topman and Miss Selfridge have performed well. The hard work in the boom years seems to have paid off, and the consolidation should reap further benefits for the group as a whole.

One of the big benefits is that Green has now appointed a Chief Executive for the merged group. Bhs hasn't had a chief executive for the past seven years and now Ian Grabiner has the role across the whole of Arcadia. There's also a new buyer across the Burton and Bhs menswear ranges. The more efficiencies of this sort, the more Green can reduce operational costs.

A GLOBAL DIMENSION

So Green has consolidated rather than expanded his business, but he has also been daring. While he does takes risks, they're calculated risks: so he must have been fairly sure that opening his long-awaited flagship Topshop store in New York during the recession would work. It was launched in April 2009 and was reported to have cost $24 million.

And, despite record high unemployment in New York, the shoppers turned up at the new store in their droves. Queues began to form at 6 a.m. on 2 April and shoppers waited five hours to buy British fashion. Kate Moss was on hand to lend glamour and support, and the opening was hailed a success.

More Topshop stores are planned for the US in places like Boston, Miami and Los Angeles. Analysts in America think it could work because people with less money to spend will try Topshop where they would have gone to the traditional big stores like Macys and Sacks. Gina Kelly, fashion director at *17* magazine, said: 'The prices are spot on. It's not expensive and they are very quick with getting the newest trends in store right away. They change their merchandise a lot and that's what American shoppers want.' [3]

Again, Green's key factors of price and speed are winning the day.

CREDIT WHERE IT'S DUE

Recession or no recession, Green's empire is too big for one man to do it all alone and he's not the only member of his team to have been working harder. My retail analyst pointed out to me, quite emphatically, that all the credit for riding out the recession in such style can't go to Green alone: 'don't forget his key cohorts, in particular Ian Grabiner'.

The hard work in the boom years seems to have paid off, and the consolidation should reap further benefits for the group as a whole.

Grabiner now has Arcadia to run, but he has already presided over the merger of Bhs and Arcadia, and the Topshop launch in New York. He's also being credited with making sure profits across the group rose in the 12 months to September 2009. If that's a foretaste of what's to come, the new enlarged Arcadia will be making headlines for some time.

While he's been lauded as the 'engine room' of Arcadia, he's said to be a tough operator – 'Grabiner's ability with numbers, and iron grasp on the operations of the business, has played a key part in Green's success.'[4] Given how hard he works, Green needs to have trusted people like Grabiner on his team. They're safe hands to leave the business in while Green takes some hard earned rest.

IT'S NOT ALL WORK AND NO PLAY

Despite the fact that Green is well-known for being 'in the office' at Bhs and Arcadia, sometimes until 1 or 2 in the morning, tinkering with displays and checking product, he loves his rest and relaxation. He admits to playing cards, a bit of tennis and table tennis, but strictly no business. The villa in Monaco is the perfect place for resting by the pool and getting away from the stresses of the recession and he has all the trappings of wealth, including the yacht, cars, helicopter and private jet.

Green's key factors of price and speed are winning the day.

While he's at work, Green works; while he's on holiday, he's resting. The two don't mix.

Of course, back in London, there's always the chance to relax on a few nights out with his friend and new business partner Simon Cowell, and Kate and the girls. Green enjoys partying and being generous to family and friends. His parties have made headlines. He was criticized in the press for his 50th birthday bash in 2002, when he flew a reported 200 guests to Cyprus from the UK for three days of the high life. More recently, the 50th birthday party he threw for Simon Cowell made headlines too.

NOT OUT OF THE WOODS

While Green is ebullient about increased profits and is planning to move into Europe, Hong Kong and even India and China with his Topshop brand, he's still realistic about the immediate future. Alan Sugar has been declaring that he's fed up with the 'R' word and that we're out of recession in the UK, but Green has been warning that 2010 will be tough for retailers and that increasing taxes and unemployment are still holding the recovery back. He told Reuters in October 2009 that recovery would be slow: 'I think it's going to be hard work ahead, a long slog … I don't see any easing in the next 12 months.'[5] He also told *Retail Week*, the trade magazine, that rising costs and the increase in VAT back to 17.5% in January 2010 would hit consumers' pockets and that confidence was low because of worries about more unemployment to come.

His sourcing and negotiating skills and his constant focus on efficiency are more important than ever.

Unemployment at the end of 2009 was still rising, and the 16–24 age bracket who use Miss Selfridge and Topshop have been badly hit. It could well be that Green's customer numbers fall if there are big job losses in the public sector. Spending cuts must be on the cards and public sector workers with their mid-range pay packets could yet be forced to go to cheaper shops like Primark and New Look. Green is realistic enough to know that he's got to keep his customers spending.

While the pound is weak, retailers have to pay more for goods from overseas; most analysts think it's impossible for retailers to keep their prices down much longer. Green's already been roundly criticized by suppliers for squeezing them yet again when Bhs merged with Arcadia and they were told to increase their discounts by 3% to match those given to Arcadia brands. Suppliers may not be able to cut costs much further.

So price rises look inevitable, despite worries that they will deter shoppers. For Green, that means pushing even harder through the tough times and doing more of what he does so well; giving his customers something special that they just have to buy at a price that they're willing and able to pay. His sourcing and negotiating skills and his constant focus on efficiency are more important than ever. Even though Alan Sugar was right and the UK was out of recession in November 2009, the effects of it are likely to be felt for a long time to come. There's still more hard work for Green and his team to do.

WHEN THE GOING GETS TOUGH – WORK HARDER!

- **Give the customer something special.** This is more important than ever in a downturn. Green knows what they'll be prepared to pay for a product but that you have to give them a valid reason to shop with you and not the competition.
- **Remember that the customer is everything.** If you don't have enough customers to generate enough to pay the loan repayments and the bills, you go out of business.
- **Profit is vanity in recession.** Break even and ride it out until the shoppers come back. Even Green views recession as a time to consolidate and if you do make a profit, it's a bonus.
- **Avoid raising your prices.** Everybody will need to tighten their belts, all along the supply chain. If you have to pass increased costs onto the customer, they'll buy less or stop buying at all. Green is constantly trying to find ways to cut costs and expects suppliers to share the pain.
- **Keep an eye out for a great deal.** Recession presents opportunities to entrepreneurs who may be able to afford to snap them up. Consolidate by all means to reduce costs, but make sure you don't overlook new prospects.

8

AIM HIGH AND KEEP TRYING

'I am brave, but I take a view. It is an educated view. I am careful. I am not reckless.' [1]

Philip Green

I n 1999, Green bought the remains of the Sears Group, broke it up and sold off the various parts. The investors, who included Tom Hunter and the Barclay Brothers, had made around £250 million from the deal.

But Green wanted to aim even higher. He made it clear that he wanted to own the biggest prize on the high street – the UK's much loved Marks and Spencer. It was much bigger than anything Green had set his sights on before but it fitted his bill: an opportunity to buy a struggling retailer for a good price, in the business he knows best, where he could use his skills to add value and keep the customers satisfied.

THE MAIN CHANCE

Marks and Spencer in 1999–2000 was struggling, but it was an altogether different proposition to the Sears Group. It was much bigger and worth a great deal more money. Green might have been fairly rich after a succession of brilliant deals, but he wasn't *that* rich! Still, he was riding high and aiming high, and he obviously believed the dizzy heights of Marks and Spencer ownership was attainable.

Marks and Spencer may have been struggling, but it was still an iconic British high street institution. It was the kind of place visitors to the UK went while they were here on holiday, in much the same way they went to the British Museum or Edinburgh Castle. And what on earth would 'someone such as Green' do with it? Break it up and sell it off in parcels? Make money out of it? It might have flaws, but they were Marks and Spencer flaws!

If he didn't break it up and sell it on he'd have to run it, and run it better than it was being run, to add value and make a profit. But

Green still hadn't much of a track record when it came to running retail businesses. All the old stories about his unsuccessful companies in his early career, and his difficulties with running a public company, were dissected again.

In January 2000 the chain's sales figures were worse than expected. Green was putting together the money for the bid and creating a big-name management team who would work with him if he was successful. There were experienced retailers on that team who would help attract other big names and important investors. Not only did Green have the pulling power to bring in key real estate partners, investors and bankers, but he could also attract key people to work with him.

Not only did Green have the pulling power to bring in key real estate partners, investors and bankers, but he could also attract key people to work with him.

While Green was preparing his bid, the Marks and Spencer board stumbled on Marks and Spencer shares owned by Tina Green. Journalists were alerted that Marks and Spencer was going to refer her share purchases to the Department of Trade and Industry to investigate. It didn't matter that Green had stuck to the letter of the law; once the headlines appeared, his bid was holed below the surface and his bid sank.

SECOND CHANCE

But Green is a restless entrepreneur who loves doing a deal, and turning around a couple of struggling retail chains like Bhs and Arcadia – while it might prove to the rest of the world he really was a brilliant retailer – wasn't enough to keep him occupied and interested. He still lusted after the big retail prize and so he had another shot at Marks and Spencer in 2004.

By this point, Green was fourth on the *Sunday Times Rich List*, with £3.6 billion. Green knew he could do for Marks and Spencer what he done for Bhs and Arcadia. The Marks and Spencer management seemed weak, the board didn't have a permanent chairman, and the shareholders were disgruntled. Green had big-name bankers supporting him like Robin Saunders, Bob Wigley and Peter Cummings, and he tried to get Stuart Rose to agree to take the top job on his management team. Rose turned him down.

Green knew he could do for Marks and Spencer what he done for Bhs and Arcadia.

As soon as the Marks and Spencer board knew that Green was serious about his bid, they sprung into action. Having prevaricated for months about appointing a new chief executive, they hired Stuart Rose and the existing incumbent Roger Holmes was given his cards. A new chairman was appointed too. It was a last-gasp attempt to keep Green out and, with a stronger management team in place, the firm's share price went up.

Green's initial bid was low and was turned down. Despite questions arising about Stuart Rose's own shareholding in Marks and Spencer (which he was later cleared of by the Financial Services Authority), the board refused Green's second and third offers. The shareholders backed the board at the AGM on 14 July 2004 and Green withdrew his bid.

BEATEN AGAIN

Green told the *Daily Mail* in 2004: 'I passionately wanted to own Marks and Spencer, but … the question was: "Do I want to win at any price?" The answer was I didn't.'[2]

So what would have been in store for Marks and Spencer had Green won the day? Fewer lines, fewer layers of management, new deals with suppliers, faster turnover of lines, more attention paid to what the customers wanted, Green walking the floors at night checking displays and ranges? He would have wanted to make Marks and Spencer into a private company. Why buy the jewel in the crown of retailing and then have a board and shareholders to tell you how to run it? As he told James Hurley of *Growing Business* in February 2009, 'I had the tools to fix it, I understood the customer and what needed to be done … we'd have done a great job.'[3] Green passionately wanted to own Marks and Spencer, and still seemed passionate – even in early 2009 – about what he could have done to fix it.

ONE MORE TIME?

My business analyst wouldn't be surprised if he tried again:

> '*He still has an interest in Marks and Spencer, but in his case it is business not personal. If an opportunity arises that he thinks is a good one, he will seriously consider if he can do the deal and go for it. If this happens with Marks and Spencer, he will be there again.*'

Whether or not Green does go for Marks and Spencer again, and even if he does and isn't successful, he's still made an impact on the giant retailer: 'If there is one big lesson of Marks and Spencer's great soap opera of city life, it is that a mature business can benefit from the threat of being taken over by a Philip Green or the institutional version – private equity. Marks and Spencer would be in a lot worse shape if it hadn't reacted to the shock of Green's attempt to buy it.'[4]

My retail analyst agrees: 'It spurred the appointment of Sir Stuart Rose who has certainly changed the culture of the business for good (probably) and for the good – unarguably.'

THE GREEN X-FACTOR

Even when he doesn't buy a business, Green's credited these days with improving it! His reputation as a retailer has come a long way. He really does seem to have the retailing X-factor.

But he's still the same character: a driven, competitive, ambitious man who can get distracted and has a phenomenal brain for figures and detail and a feel for what the customer wants. In common with other retailers in the UK, he's been rather preoccupied with steering his fleet of ships through the current economic choppy waters, but, as the UK slowly emerges from recession, can we expect him to take a back seat, retire to Monaco and drift into obscurity always wishing he'd bagged Marks and Spencer? Not a chance!

PASTURES NEW

Green is amusing himself with a new venture with his friend Simon Cowell. They've set up a TV production, talent management and merchandising company. They're reported at the time of writing to be in talks with Kate Moss to get her on board too. It's been called a £1 billion 'Disney style entertainment empire' with Kate Moss as the figurehead and style setter for the fashion end of the business.

This is a departure for Green. It's the first time he'll have started a business with a business partner and gone outside his comfort zone of the fashion industry. Up until now he has stuck with what he knows. That's been one of his rules. But he does take risks – calculated risks – so we can be sure that he has worked out how the business will fare in the worst-case scenario and is convinced it can succeed. The inclusion of Kate Moss on the team would suggest an element of fashion will be involved and Green certainly knows that business through and through.

Green has also declared his intention to expand the Topshop chain into Europe and China and to launch more stores in the US. With all that going on, he certainly will have to go on working harder.

TRY, TRY, TRY AGAIN?

With profits at Arcadia up despite the recession, and Ian Grabiner at the helm with the brief of overseeing the day-to-day management of the business, is the famously hands-on Green stepping back just to concentrate on Topshop's expansion and his new business with Simon Cowell? Or is there another motive?

The merger of Bhs into Arcadia is almost complete. Topshop is doing very well, as is Topman. Evans, Wallis and Dorothy Perkins are probably doing as well as can be expected under the circumstances, in common with other ranges in the mid-market, but Green's hoping that sales can be revitalized. Dorothy Perkins clothes are making the pages of the fashion mags, and the chain has a new Dorothy Perkins Limited range and is selling a small selection of brands. He'll also be hoping that Yasmin Le Bon and Beth Ditto can do for Wallis and Evans what Kate Moss has done for Topshop.

For the fourth year in a row Green hasn't paid himself a dividend and has concentrated on reducing the group's debt and remodelling the stores, but he dismisses the idea that any of this might be in preparation for finding a buyer for Arcadia.

At the time of writing, journalists have reported in various interviews that he thinks that Christmas 2009 will be downbeat and too early to tell if the economy has touched bottom. His views seem to be borne out by various surveys that show unemployment is the spectre that still worries a lot of people for the New Year, and they're saving rather than spending.

'Marks and Spencer would be in a lot worse shape if it hadn't reacted to the shock of Green's attempt to buy it.' [4]

Whatever 2010 brings, people will still be asking the same question. Surely the high street emperor has another trick up his sleeve? The Marks and Spencer share price is well under the £4-a-share ceiling Green imposed on his last bid in 2004 and Stuart Rose is set to leave the business in 2010 to be replaced as Chief Executive by Marc Bolland, who is credited with turning round the Morrisions supermarket chain. Will this appointment of Marc Bolland put the cat among the pigeons? Is another stab at Marks and Spencer out of the question? My retail analyst thinks not: 'There is no plan B. He would see it as his crowning glory.'

CHANGING TIMES

The deal would cost less than in 2004 with the share price well down, but it's not only share prices that have changed. Marks and Spencer has changed too. There were several high profile candidates for the job of Chief Executive who pulled out of the race because they didn't want it. The Marks and Spencer job is no longer seen as the top job in retailing and some of those approached felt they already have better jobs. Marks and Spencer doesn't have the prestige it once had. Would Green be able to put together the kind of top-level management team he'd need?

The whole face of banking has changed dramatically too. Money is harder to come by and Green's main backer Peter Cummings has fallen off his HBOS perch. Still, if Green decides to go for it, he won't let that stop him. He never seems to give up or take no for an answer, he hasn't done a deal in a while, he's restless, and has boundless energy so he'll have already thought all that through – just in case!

Is another stab at Marks and Spencer out of the question?

There's just no one like him in UK retailing, but there is one person who sounds as if she'd like Green to slow down a bit. In the words of his daughter Chloe Green, reported in *The Sunday Times* in November 2009: 'I'm so glad he didn't buy Marks and Spencer, though now he's started a new venture with Simon Cowell. It's exciting, but hard work. I've seen him getting stressed – probably because he's working with someone else. He's never done that before.'[6]

AIM HIGH AND KEEP TRYING

- **Add value when you can.** Even if you are a small fish in a big pond – if you think you can add value, go for it. Green has the skills to add the kind of value to a business that means he can sell at a good profit.
- **Learn from your mistakes.** You have to really, really want something for it to succeed but if it doesn't, don't see it as a failure; learn from it and try again. Green didn't treat his first unsuccessful bid for Marks and Spencer as failure; he just bought Bhs and Arcadia and tried again. Each time he's learned about putting together the finances and the people for a big takeover.
- **Be prepared to walk away.** If you find it's going to cost you too much or you're not getting what you thought you were getting, pull out. Green did this during his second Marks and Spencer bid when he realized that he wasn't getting all the information he needed.
- **Keep trying.** If you're meant to have it, another chance will come along and not getting something can leave you in a better position to go for an even better opportunity that presents itself. Green ended up better off financially as a result of not buying Marks and Spencer, as his success at Bhs made him his first billion pounds.
- **Work with what you have.** Aim high with the businesses you have as well as the ones you'd like to have. Green aimed and succeeded in taking Topshop to the top and is rolling it out as a global brand.

9

STAY PRIVATE, BUT ENJOY THE PUBLICITY

'The difference about Philip is that he plays with his own money, not a plc's money. He puts his balls on the table every time and that's what you've got to admire about him.'[1]

Marco Pierre White, chef and restaurateur

G reen presides over the biggest private retail business in the UK. By taking Bhs and Arcadia into private ownership, Green makes the decisions about how an eighth of the UK clothing market is run. For someone who started in the wholesale shoe trade at 15 with not a single qualification to his name, it must be a very pleasing thought. Not only has he defied his detractors and the doubters who said he doesn't have what it takes to be a credible retailer, but he's turned out to be a brilliant one, who has beaten them all at their own game.

But while being 'private' in business terms has been to Green's advantage, he's developed a healthy respect for the power of publicity. Few business people make the impact Green makes in the press and media, and each quote or appearance is accompanied by the name of at least one of his chains, keeping them firmly in the public eye.

PRIVATE GREEN

Apart from his attempts to buy Marks and Spencer, the last time Green dabbled in a public company with a board and shareholders was when he ran Amber Day. The experience was to imprint itself in such a way that he vowed to reporters at the time that he'd never to run a publicly listed company again.

Green likes to do things his own way. One of his most significant traits is speed: the speed of the decision-making process, leading to the speed with which he does deals, turns around ailing retailing groups and sells them on, as well as his understanding of the need for speed in the supply chain and the turnover of the lines in his stores. He can't abide having to wait around for others to make decisions. He has to be fast and flexible to keep ahead of the competition. The last thing he needs is to be hampered and held back by the committee decision-making process – the board that has to discuss and debate the new proposals, and deliberate on the next move, or the shareholders who have a vote before a particular plan can be implemented.

Green makes the decisions about how an eighth of the UK high street is run.

Given his past decisions, Green has always seemed to prefer to find the money himself or to raise funds from bankers and friends – clearing any debts as quickly as possible so as to be unopposed at the helm. The relatively low interest rates of the last 15 years have made it cheaper to raise the money and service the debts, so it's been a good time to be private.

Because the firms are his own, Green is also able to borrow, to take large amounts of cash out of them in the form of dividends, without waiting for a board to approve those dividends. Whether he buys a business to grow it and invest in it or to make a short-term killing is his decision alone. It's much harder for someone running a public company to sell off assets and make staff redundant, but that can hold the business back and slow down its ability to keep up with the competition and change with the demands of the customers – to the point where it's vulnerable to private takeover.

PROFITABLE PRIVACY

Not only does Green prefer to own his own companies without interference from investors, but he's made more money from owning private firms. His genius has been to buy a firm when the shares are falling, the management weak and the shareholders dissatisfied.

In the 1990s, UK Retailing plc was in pretty poor shape and there were plenty of such firms for Green to choose from. The underlying value of the businesses he bought was such that someone with Green's talents could snap up a bargain, add value fairly easily and sell for a big profit. If you do your sums right, you may also acquire a fair chunk of valuable property against which you can raise additional finance, if you need it, for further acquisitions or expansions. And you can go ahead with your plans without having to sell off shares to demanding shareholders, who appoint a chairman and board to oversee all of your decisions, on their behalf.

He can't abide having to wait around for others to make decisions.

When Green was learning his trade and doing deals in the early part of his career, he was surrounded by revered public retailing firms and his role models would have been the chairmen of those groups. They were the famous retailers of the day like Sir Charles Clore who owned, through Sears Holdings, the British Shoe Corporation and Selfridges department store, as well as investing in property, and Sir Ralph Halpern, Chairman of the Burton Group.

But Green seems to have started a trend for private ownership. Many public firms in the UK have gone private including the massive Alliance Boots pharmacy chain and New Look. But apart from Green's there are few big retailers owned by individual entrepreneurs. Most are owned by private equity firms who have appointed chief executives to run their acquisitions – people with undoubtedly great retailing skills and experience, but few who have made much personal impact.

THE PRIVATE LIFE FOR ME

Another pleasing aspect of owning and running your own private concern is that you don't have to care much what the City thinks: there are no share prices to go up and down in value, reflecting what the City makes of every decision you take. The appointment of a new chief executive doesn't make much real difference to the value of the firm in terms of share prices, but it can make a huge difference to your profits and the appointment is down to you – not a board. There's no board to tell you on behalf of shareholders that you're not doing the job well and so it's time you left. The downside is that if you run out of cash there are no shareholders to ask for more to bail you out and if the banks aren't lending, you can be in for a tough time.

Green seems to have started a trend for private ownership.

Green seems to operate better when he has the freedom to make the tough decisions quickly – decisions that he feels have to be made to turn a struggling company into a top performer. He can pay over the odds to get and keep the best staff. He is in control and he seems to like it that way. He alone decides his business objectives, unless he cares to ask for advice.

ON THE PUBLIC STAGE

While Green wants privacy to get on with running his businesses his own way, he also actively courts publicity. He's not above announcing his firm's profits to the press when he wants to impress with his retailing skills. A year after he took over at Bhs, he announced that the ailing firm was flourishing and in profit to the tune of £31.5

million. A year later he announced that profits were around three times that at £100.2 million and the loans had been paid off.

2002 was quite a year for Green. He turned 50 in March and had the kind of birthday event that keeps the press mesmerized for months. There was a host of celebrity guests and family, an exclusive hotel in Cyprus, togas, champagne, and days of partying. Then he moved up the *Sunday Times Rich List* to number 13 with £1.2 billion in the bank, due to the dramatic increase in value of Bhs in just two years. And profits at the firm had trebled. Less than ten years previously, he'd been worth mere millions.

And he does announce falls in profit too. In November 2005 he was reported on fashionunited.co.uk as saying profits at Bhs were expected to fall by at least 30%: 'Sales are down, product is off the boil and I am happy to fix it … when you get the product wrong, you get punished … I am happy to take ownership of it.'[2]

TURNING THE GOSSIP COLUMNS GREEN

Green has become a celebrity in his own right, in the gossip columns as much as in the business pages.

Associations with celebrities like Kate Moss and Simon Cowell have launched Green into an altogether higher publicity sphere. There's hardly a report about an A-list party or a big charity fundraising event worth the name that doesn't have a line about Philip Green and who he had on his arm or what he spent. There's little need to spend vast sums of hard-earned profit on advertising when the papers regularly give Green a name-check and add 'owner of Topshop and Dorothy Perkins'.

REWARDS

Publicity is all very well. Having the cameras popping everywhere you go is fun. But you know you've 'arrived' in any profession if your peers are heaping awards for greatness upon you.

The retail industry is no different. Your profits, requests for your considered opinion, and gold-embossed invitations are as nothing compared to the plaudits of your rivals and competitors. They know how great you've had to be, the adversity you've faced, the time and resources you've had to expend to get where you are today, and if they say you're the best then you truly are the best. And of course in turn each award or reward is likely to generate yet more publicity, which is great for the business.

AWARDS

Despite the reservations that Green inspires, he's not been short of those coveted retailing awards. He was given the Retail Personality of the Year award in 2002 by *Retail Week*. It is the retailing version of the Oscars and he was understandably delighted. He won it again in 2003. No one had ever won it two years in a row.

In 2004, Green made the grade as the most influential person in high street fashion. It was the year he made his second bid for Marks and Spencer and reached the dizzy heights of number four in the *Sunday Times Rich List*. He was also named 'the entrepreneurs' entrepreneur' by the Confederation of British Industry. In 2005 he rewarded himself and his family with the huge £1.2 billion dividend from Arcadia and announced that he was putting £5 million aside to set up his Fashion Retail Academy.

KNIGHTHOOD

In June 2006 Green got the award he had probably long been hoping for – his knighthood. It was awarded to him for services to retail in the Queen's 80th Birthday Honours List and he was one of few businesspeople on the list. While Green would have clearly been over the moon, his detractors were appalled. Why, when he was paying big dividends to the owner of Arcadia – his wife, who lived in Monaco, thus not paying UK tax on it – should he get a knighthood? His friends argued that he deserved it, had had a big hand in revitalizing the UK high street and had helped to create huge wealth in the UK.

Green seems to operate better when he has the freedom to make the tough decisions quickly.

Whichever side of that debate you take, Green would have been happy with the knighthood and taken it as recognition by the establishment that he had the retail world at his feet.

HALL OF FAME

In 2008 another honour came Green's way when he was inducted into the World Retail Hall of Fame. The World Retail Congress, the representative body for retailers globally, launched the Hall of Fame in 2007 to recognize the contribution to the industry of key individuals. Anita Roddick, Laura Ashley and Giorgio Armani were on the list of 100 original members. Green's induction took place in Barcelona in April 2008. Andrew Davidson, who interviewed him in March 2008 for *The Times*, said: 'Don't underestimate how chuffed he is. And that counts because Green is a bundle of insecurities, like most of us ...he and his wife already sit on a fortune of almost £5 billion. Yet still he worries about how the rest of us rate him.'[3]

THE BUSINESS GURU

Green's been there, run the companies, gained the fame and won the medals. He has the financial rewards and over the last couple of years, his views on business issues have been widely sought. He's been regularly quoted on the recession, its impact and the possible long-term effects on the high street and the labour market. He may be increasingly seen as a celebrity worthy of the glossy magazines, for himself rather than just his clothes, but he's also increasingly taken seriously on the business stage.

Green's new ventures in the States have also allowed him centre stage there. His new business with Cowell assures him of many more headlines to come and with the impending global domination of Topshop he's heading for world stardom.

There's little doubt he loves the attention; all the more reason to think that he's unlikely to give it all up and retire to the beaches of Monaco for a while yet.

In 2008 another honour came Green's way when he was inducted into the World Retail Hall of Fame.

And he has that vast personal fortune on hand to help him finance the next big deal. With Green, there's always a next big deal – so don't despair, the Green light isn't likely to go out of our lives any time soon.

STAY PRIVATE, BUT ENJOY THE PUBLICITY

- **Be open where you can be.** If you own your own business, the lines of reporting are less onerous and you can keep many of the details of your business figures to yourself. Green does announce his figures and because he's such a well-known retailer, they attract publicity.
- **Stay nimble in making decisions.** When there's only you in charge, you can make decisions much more quickly to get on and make things happen. If you have to refer to the board and shareholders, you can be slowed down to the detriment of the business. Green is quick at making decisions and they are his alone.
- **Find good advisors.** It can be quite isolating running a business otherwise. Green does have friends and trusted advisers on his company board.
- **Have a plan for tough times.** Green is the master of raising any money he needs for his business, so he's happy being private. But private companies can run into financial problems when times are hard and there's no one to ask for help in raising more cash.
- **Make the most of free publicity.** Getting yourself and your firm some publicity can be worth thousands of pound of advertising – as long as it's not bad publicity. Green knows it can pay to be in the limelight. Whether the story is about him or some aspect of how he runs his business, his brands get named and noticed.
- **Aim for awards and accolades.** Not only will they prove you're at the top of your game but, as Green knows, they also generate publicity and are likely to increase the public's respect.

10
GIVE SOMETHING BACK

'Philanthropy is the only motivator to continue making money.'[1]

Sir Tom Hunter, Green's friend and business associate

Although money has always been a motivating factor for Green and he is committed to making it, he makes a point of giving something back – to good causes and to the industry itself.

He is one of the UK's major philanthropists. He's not quite a self-made man, having been left some money by his entrepreneurial father. But money is a driving factor for him and, in the course of his career, he has made the kind of money most people and indeed most entrepreneurs can't even imagine. On the 2009 *Sunday Times Rich List* Green is the UK's sixth richest man – up from ninth the previous year, despite estimates that his personal fortune has fallen from around £4.3 billion to £3.83 billion. He's one of the lucky ones; his fortune hasn't been badly hit during the current recession due to the nature of his investments.

Times are hard! The *Rich List* shows that the UK's richest 1000 are collectively worth £155 billion less in 2009 than a year earlier. The number of billionaires has fallen from 75 to 43. It's the biggest annual fall since the list began 21 years ago. For some charities and good causes, that will lead to a fall in the donations they get. But Green seems to be carrying on with his support for various good causes.

FLASH THE CASH

So what do you do with almost £4 billion? As well as looking after your family and thinking about the future, you might give money to charity. Green gives millions away every year.

In 2007 the chief executive of Jewish Care, the largest health and social care charity for the Jewish community in London, announced at the end of a fundraising dinner that Philip Green was continuing his support of the organization by giving the charity a £1 million donation each year for the next five years. Another of his charities is the Retail Trust, which supports people who work in or are retired from the retail sector and need help or assistance. Green pledged £150,000 to the trust at the annual dinner in January 2009.

His fortune hasn't been badly hit during the current recession due to the nature of his investments.

Green is regularly seen at the top charity dinners and balls, and often leads the bidding at charity auctions or gives the biggest donation at a charity fundraising event. In November 2009, while this book was being written, his name cropped up several times at high-profile charity events. One of them was the Krug Mindshare charity auction. Simon Cowell raised £19,000 for charity Children's Hospice after donating one hour of his time through Krug Mindshare – a unique campaign that aims to raise money for charity through businessmen and women auctioning their time. His hour was bought by Lucian Grange, CEO of Universal Music. An hour with Green went for £18,000.

At the 2008 Music Industry Trusts' Awards at London's Grosvenor House Hotel, the charity bidders made more headlines than the award winners. Bono of U2 and Green pushed up the bidding for a box at Arsenals' Emirates Stadium to £21,000, with Bono winning. Green paid £6000 to meet Lionel Ritchie. But the top lot of the night was a guitar made for and signed by Bono. Green bought that for £150,000!

But one charity auction stands out above all others in impact. At Annabel's nightclub in 2006, Green paid £60,000 to kiss Kate Moss. He handed the prize to Jemima Khan and the minute-long smooch that resulted made more headlines than a royal wedding. Indirectly it's been making headlines for Green ever since. The model and the mogul have been working together ever since: the ranges continue to make headlines and their frequent outings when Green is in London also get them in the gossip columns. You can't pay for publicity like that.

So what do you do with almost £4 billion?

After the tsunami hit on Boxing Day 2004 and people in south-east Asia lost everything, Green was quick off the mark with £100,000 in cash and £1 million worth of clothes. When Madeline McCann went missing in Portugal in 2007, he immediately offered money for a reward for information and later offered his private jet to take her parents to meet the Pope.

GOOD CAUSES

Green has other causes that he funds for the good of the fashion industry itself. In 2005 he bemoaned the lack of talent in UK fashion and announced he was setting up an academy to teach 16- to 18-year-olds fundamental skills needed by the industry, such as design, IT, technology, marketing and buying.

He gave £5 million to setting up the Fashion Retail Academy. It takes in 60 students a year and has around 350 in total. Green told the BBC in March 2005 that the aim was to promote fashion retail as a career and that it would nurture 'entrepreneurial talents through both unique behind the scenes insight and direct contact with industry leaders.'[2]

The academy opened in September 2006 with 200 students who work for a diploma in fashion retail. They spend almost as much time working on the shop floor as in the classroom, with work experience across all areas of retailing: buying, visual merchandising and distribution. Marks and Spencer, Tesco, and Next are also involved in the project, and Green told *The Daily Telegraph* when it opened: 'My hope is that this will be a flagship for other industries … Training people and bringing through a new generation of people is paramount to the future success of retailing in the UK. We can develop people who love this business and have a passion for it in their blood.'[3]

Green does his bit for the academy with money and master classes. But of course, he's a winner too, in that he'll have students on work experience and potential recruits to work in his business after they graduate. Everyone wins. He's also given £1.25 million for 50 schools to become specialists in teaching business.

Green has other causes that he funds for the good of the fashion industry itself.

Apart from the academy, Green also sponsors the New Generation programme for young up-and-coming designers. Kate Moss isn't the only designer to get space on Topshop's rails; the NewGen programme, which is part of London Fashion Week, brings young designers into the business. Chosen designers get £100,000, which helps to pay for the production of a sample collection and a show. Topshop is repaid with spin-off collections for its shop rails. Christopher Kane is the latest – he was given as much retailing space as Kate Moss this season and his is the highest-profile post-sponsorship relationship to date. The collaborations raise the profile of the retailer, attract new customers, the designers get exposure to a mass audience and shoppers get designer clothes at affordable prices. Again, everyone wins.

GRABBING OPPORTUNITIES FOR GIVING

It's all high-profile stuff and better for Green's brands than any advertising. Here's an entrepreneur who is giving something back to the industry and to young people who want to work in the industry. This is job creation for the good of the whole of UK Ltd.

Green also sponsors the new generation programme for young up-and-coming designers.

But Green is always quick to spot extra opportunities. While speaking at the University of Oxford's Said Business School one evening in 2005, a student asked whether, if he had a good business idea, Green or his fellow speaker would back it. Green asked the audience for a show of hands from those who thought they had good business ideas. When dozens of hands went up, he announced that he would put up £500,000 for the best ideas and persuaded his fellow speaker to match his offer. Along with a third businessman, who put up another £1 million, they came up with a ten-year project – the Said Business School Venture Fund – which gives away £200,000 a year to students with the best business ideas.

GREEN'S GIVING

You could be forgiven for thinking that a lot of publicity attends some of Green's generosity, that he has an eye for a high-profile giving opportunity. Some of his charity giving seems to be done very publicly. It could be that he's just a very spontaneous person, who reacts as the need arises. It could be that, as in business, he's always quick to spot a good opportunity, and acts on it before anyone else gets in there and beats him to it. Either way, he seems to enjoy the publicity that attends his fundraising endeavours and the publicity he generates in turn raises awareness of his causes.

One of Green's first lessons was learning that the best deal is one where every party gets something out of it. The same can be said for supporting good causes in the retail field. Everything Green sets his mind to he wants to be best at, aims high and does it his own way. He does the same when giving something back by setting up something as significant as the Fashion Retail Academy. He's also competitive, and that probably leads him to keep bidding against fellow entrepreneurs at charity auctions.

Everything Green sets his mind to he wants to be best at, aims high and does it his own way.

Green is forever on the lookout for opportunities and this seems to include opportunities to set up important charitable projects. Even when he's working hard at running his business, he can still find time for good causes. And as we've seen, he wants to be liked – and what better way of doing that is to give some of your hard-earned millions to deserving charities? It's all part of the mindset that's made him one of the UK's leading entrepreneurs and richest men.

GIVE SOMETHING BACK

- **Support your favourite charities.** It's one way of giving something back. Green has quite a few that he gives to regularly.
- **Help other people gain skills.** Give money to causes that will help the sector you work in: help people to gain the skills they need to find jobs in your sector and, as Green knows, help the business people to find skilled staff they need to grow their businesses.
- **The best donations are ones where all sides benefit.** As in any other aspect of business, the best donations are ones where all sides benefit. If Green's generosity attracts publicity for his business, that's a welcome by-product.
- **Spot new ways to give something back.** There will always be different opportunities that you haven't thought of. Green sees those opportunities in the way he spots money-making opportunities.
- **Aim high with your good causes.** Green would like to see his retail academy template rolled out to other industries.
- **Keep a commitment to making money.** The more you make the more you can afford to give back.
- **Do it your way.** Come up with good ideas for projects that will benefit people. Green does his philanthropic work like he runs the rest of his business – his way.

HOW TO RUN A BUSINESS THE PHILIP GREEN WAY

1   DO IT YOUR OWN WAY

It's the only way you can do it. You are who you are. For some people like Green, that means never taking no for an answer, identi-
fying the goal and heading straight for it. Green spots an opportunity and acts fast before anyone else beats him to it. He knows
his strengths and applies them to every business opportunity. He
sticks to what he knows, which is fashion retailing, and he works
out the worst-case scenario – what if it went wrong – before he
takes the risk.

2   MAKE THE BUSINESS RUN AS EFFICIENTLY AS POSSIBLE

Even in the good times when all around you are spending money
on big overheads and unnecessary layers of management, look for
places in your operation where you can reduce costs. If you run a
lean, efficient operation, you'll be better placed to survive when
the next economic downturn strikes, as it surely will.

3   KEEP THE CUSTOMER SATISFIED

Work out how much customers will pay for your product and then
negotiate the deals that allow you to sell the product for that price
while making you as healthy a profit as possible. Customers want
a good shopping experience as well as quality products.

4   WHATEVER YOU DO, DON'T BREAK THE SUPPLY CHAIN

Everyone has to work to keep costs and ultimately prices down, including the manufacturers and suppliers. If the prices go too high, customers go elsewhere. If one supplier goes to the wall, there will always be others who want to get their goods into your shops and will do the deals – but if you have a supplier who understands your brand and would be hard to replace, you have to form a relationship and nurture it.

5   PEOPLE MATTER – YOU CAN'T RUN AN EMPIRE WITHOUT THEM

The bigger the operation, the more people you'll need and you want the best talent you can attract. You can pay over the odds and give bonuses where they're earned, but money isn't the only way to motivate people. If you give them responsibility and autonomy to use their talents, they stay with you. If you're an inspirational boss they may look for bigger challenges outside your organization, but you may attract them back when you need them.

6   SPOT THE MONEY-MAKING OPPORTUNITY

If you spot a great opportunity and are sure it will work, others will be willing to lend you the money you need. But the deal is more likely to be done if there's something in it for all parties. Investors will want a good return for their faith in you. By keeping costs down you can repay your debts quickly and use profits to grow the business.

7   WHEN THE GOING GETS TOUGH – WORK HARDER!

You need to be really focused and immerse yourself in the details of your business. The better you know your products, the more chance you have of getting the best deals from suppliers and giving the customers what they want. You need to work harder at keeping your customers happy, especially in tough economic times.

8   AIM HIGH AND KEEP TRYING

Be the best you know you can be. By looking for new challenges you will push yourself to bigger and better things, and keep your restless entrepreneurial spirit occupied. If you miss out on something you really wanted, don't think back to what you've lost. Move on. If you find something you always wanted isn't the deal you'd expected, walk away.

9   STAY PRIVATE, BUT ENJOY THE PUBLICITY

By keeping your business in private ownership, you can make things happen: you will be able to respond quicker to the changing business climate and changing customer demands. There's no committee or shareholders to keep happy. But being in the public eye pays, in that customers are more aware of you and what you have to offer.

10 GIVE SOMETHING BACK

Charity and good causes are good for you, your business and the wider community, and they bring their own rewards. You can do it your own way by coming up with new projects to put your money into, or contribute to building up skills in your own industry. Making money and giving something back aren't incompatible – the richer you become, the more you can give back.

THE LAST WORD

Where would we be without Philip Green? Retailing has rarely had someone so high profile and colourful. He's driven the resurgence of the high street, pioneered shopping as an experience, promoted UK fashion overseas as well as in the UK, and led the rush to return public companies to private ownership.

His high profile pays its own dividends in terms of publicity for his brands. Topshop especially has benefited from his thorough attention to detail. His determination to give customers what they want, along with the store's ethos of customer service, innovation, theatre and spectacle, has made it a destination in its own right – especially at the flagship store in London. Customer loyalty is important to any brand; it's less expensive to keep customers coming back and Green understands that as the master of generating customer loyalty.

Despite perceptions of Green being hard to work with, there are people who have worked with him for years, or on and off over the years. These must be strong people themselves, able to stand up to the boss and challenge him, or the relationships wouldn't last. Green appreciates those strong characters and understands the positive impact they have on his own performance, challenging him to improve and constantly innovate. And that innovation, coupled with his enthusiasm for fashion and design, especially at the iconic Topshop, has made him an employer of choice for talented young designers and buyers, so he can take his pick.

Insecurity seems to feed Green's drive for retailing supremacy and his meticulous attention to detail. But he also has an astonishing knowledge of his product. Big companies are often run by people who understand how to run a company regardless of whether they have any real knowledge of the product. Green is a product man first and foremost. He's stuck with what he knows for almost 40 years and the longer he's worked in fashion, the better he knows it.

The recession of 2008/9 is still making its mark. Before the banking crisis we were all convinced that some things are just too big to fail; what happened to the banks proved that theory wrong. Green's sheer mass of outlets and low level of debt, along with the efficiency with which he runs his operations and his customer loyalty, will all see him through. But if, instead of slowly recovering, the UK were to go back into recession (as some analysts still seem to fear at the time of writing), and inflation forces retailers to push up prices, it's not inconceivable that Green's profits could slow. If that happens, other big retailers will struggle and become vulnerable to takeover. The £4 billion Green has been saving for a rainy day could come in useful for picking up a bargain. My retail analyst says that 'the future's Green, but is it Philip Green?' It could well be – we certainly haven't heard the last of him yet.

NOTES

THE LIFE AND TIMES OF PHILIP GREEN

1   Interview with a fashion analyst, November 2009.
2   Levin, Angela, 'Don't write me off, says Philip Green', *Daily Mail*, 20 July 2004.

CHAPTER ONE

1   Danaher, Tim, 'Retail day: Green day', *Retail Week,* 22 October 2009.
2   Randall, Jeff, 'The brilliant deal-doer behind Bhs', bbc.co.uk/business, 17 January 2002.

CHAPTER TWO

1   Hurley, James, 'Sir Philip Green', *Growing Business Online*, 1 February 2009.
2   Cope, Nigel, 'Philip Green pays £200 million for Bhs chain', *The Independent*, 28 March 2000.
3   Lansley, Stewart and Forrester, Andy, *Topman: How Philip Green Built His High Street Empire*, Arum Press, 2006
4   Fletcher, Richard, 'The Bhs bonanza', *The Daily Telegraph*, 14 July 2002.
5   Randall, Jeff, 'The brilliant deal-doer behind Bhs', bbc.co.uk/business, 17 January 2002.
6   Walsh, Fiona, 'You name it we got it wrong. Wrong fashions, wrong shapes, wrong sizes', *The Guardian*, 30 September 2006.

CHAPTER THREE

1   Hall, Amanda, 'Cover story: Philip Green Live – "Katie!!"', *Real Business* 30 August 2007.

2   Rushton, Suzie, 'Philip Green: The king of the high street in his most outspoken interview ever', *The Independent,* 5 July 2007.

3   Vernon, Polly, 'Three out of five women are in love with Philip Green. Well, his shops anyway', *The Observer*, 11 February 2007.

CHAPTER FOUR

1   Interview with a business analyst, November 2009.

2   Clack, David, 'Top dollar: Sir Philip Green's celebrity CV', fhm.com, 24 October 2008.

3   Berwin, Lisa, 'Anger from Bhs suppliers as Sir Philip Green tightens terms', *Retail Week*, 26 May 2009.

4   Shields, Amy, 'Between a rock and a hard place', *Retail Week*, 5 June 2009.

CHAPTER FIVE

1   Hall, Amanda, 'Cover story: Philip Green live – "Katie!!"', *Real Business* 30 August 2007.

2   Anonymous, 'When Kate met Philip: Green reveals the story behind Moss' Topshop deal', *Daily Mail,* 30 April 2007.

CHAPTER SIX

1   Peston, Robert, *Who Runs Britain?*, Hodder and Stoughton, 2008.

CHAPTER SEVEN

1   Davey, James, 'Philip Green says market rebound overdone', reuters.com, 22 October 2009.
2   Brown, Jessica, 'Sir Philip Green to share tips on how retailers can beat the recession', drapersonline.com, 2 March 2009.
3   Anonymous, 'After all the New York parties Kate Moss gets what she really wants … a pizza', *Daily Mail*, 3 April 2009.
4   Berwin, Lisa, 'Ian Grabiner has been key to Arcadia's success', *Retail Week*, 30 October 2009.
5   Davey, James, 'Philip Green says market rebound overdone', reuters.com, 22 October 2009.

CHAPTER EIGHT

1   Davidson, Andrew, 'The Andrew Davidson interview: Philip Green', *Sunday Times*, 24 October 2004.
2   Levin, Angela, 'Don't write me off, says Philip Green', *Daily Mail*, 20 July 2004.
3   Hurley, James, 'Sir Philip Green', *Growing Business Online*, 1 February 2009.
4   Peston, Robert, *Who Runs Britain?*, Hodder and Stoughton, 2008.
5   Fox, Sue, 'Relative values: Philip Green and his daughter Chloe', *The Sunday Times*, 1 November 2009.

CHAPTER NINE

1   Anonymous, 'Profile: Philip Green: the fastest billionaire is on his Marks', timesonline.co.uk, 30 May 2004.
2   Anonymous, 'Green predicts Bhs profits drop', Fashionunited. co.uk, 16 November 2005.
3   Davidson, Andrew, 'Sir Philip Green steps into hall of fame', *The Sunday Times*, 2 March 2008.

CHAPTER TEN

1   Webster, George and Davies, Sophie, 'The *IoS* happy list 2008 – the 100', *The Independent on Sunday*, 27 April 2008.
2   Anonymous, 'Green starts £20m fashion academy', bbc.co.uk, 22 March 2005.
3   Fletcher, Richard, '"Sharp kids" who can show Sir Philip Green a thing or two', *The Daily Telegraph*, 20 September 2006.

READING LIST

Anonymous, 'The rise of the retail king: Philip Green', mycomeup. com.

Anonymous, 'Days of anger, shouting, abuse and threats', *The Guardian*, 4 March 2003.

Anonymous, 'Uncovered: Green's empress of Arcadia', *Mail on Sunday*/thisismoney.co.uk, 23 March 2003.

Anonymous, 'Brain food: How he made his pile – Phillip Green', *Management Today*, 1 December 2003.

Anonymous, 'Profile: Philip Green: the fastest billionaire is on his Marks', timesonline.co.uk, 30 May 2004.

Anonymous, 'Philip Green and Ruth Kelly launch the Fashion Retail Academy', trainingreference.co.uk, 25 March 2005.

Anonymous, 'When Kate met Philip: Green reveals the story behind Moss' Topshop deal', *Daily Mail*, 30 April 2007.

Anonymous, 'Arcadia merges Burton and Bhs menswear role', *Retail Week*, 25 September 2009.

Berwin, Lisa, 'Anger from Bhs suppliers as Sir Philip Green tightens terms', *Retail Week*, 26 May 2009.

Berwin, Lisa, 'Sir Philip Green outlines plans for Bhs merger with Arcadia', *Drapers/Retail Week*, 6 July 2009.

Berwin, Lisa, 'Will Arcadia's Cinderellas come to the ball?' *Drapers/ Retail Week*, 22 October 2009.

Blackhurst, Chris and Tomkinson, Martin, 'Emperor in new clothes (*corrected*)', *The Independent*, 27 September 1992.

Brown, Jessica, 'Sir Philip Green to share tips on how retailers can beat the recession', drapersonline.com, 2 March 2009.

Brummer, Alex, 'All change as Green shakes up his empire', *Daily Mail*, 15 July 2009.

Bumpus, Jessica, 'Daughter designer', *Vogue*, 2 November 2009.

Bumpus, Jessica, 'A piece of my mind', *Vogue*, 3 November 2009.

Clack, David, 'Top dollar: Sir Philip Green's celebrity CV', fhm.com, 24 October 2008.

Clark, Andrew, 'Friendly advice from Sir Philip Green', *The Guardian*, 2 April 2009.

Clark, Andrew, 'Topshop bites into the Big Apple', The Guardian, 2 April 2009.

Danaher, Tim, 'Arcadia profits soar', *Retail Week*, 22 October 2009.

Danaher, Tim, 'Retail day: Green day', *Retail Week*, 22 October 2009.

Danaher, Tim, 'Fewer, bigger stores for Arcadia as profits soar', *Retail Week*, 23 October 2009.

Davey, James, 'Philip Green says market rebound overdone', reuters.com, 22 October 2009.

Davidson, Andrew, 'The Andrew Davidson interview: Philip Green', *The Sunday Times*, 24 October 2004.

Davidson, Andrew, 'Sir Philip Green steps into hall of fame', *The Sunday Times*, 2 March 2008.

Dowell, Ben, 'Simon Cowell and Philip Green in talks to set up joint talent firm', *The Guardian*, 24 June 2009.

Finch, Julia, 'Philip Green pays himself record £1.2bn', *The Guardian*, 21 October 2005.

Fletcher, Richard, 'The Bhs bonanza', *The Daily Telegraph*, 14 July 2002.

Fletcher, Richard, '"Sharp kids" who can show Sir Philip Green a thing or two', *The Daily Telegraph*, 20 September 2006.

Hall, Amanda, 'Cover story: Philip Green live – "Katie!!"', *Real Business* 30 August 2007.

Hall, James, 'Sir Philip Green to merge Arcadia and Bhs', *The Daily Telegraph*, 25 February 2009.

Hickman, Martin, 'Sir Philip and the biggest pay cut in history', The Independent, 27 October 2006.

Hurley, James, 'Sir Philip Green', *Growing Business Online*, 1 February 2009.

Lansley, Stewart and Forrester, Andy, *Topman: How Philip Green Built His High Street Empire*, Arum Press, 2006.

Laurance, Ben, 'M&S's maverick shopper', *The Observer*, 30 January 2000.

Levin, Angela, 'Don't write me off, says Philip Green', *Daily Mail*, 20 July 2004.

MacDonald, George, 'Sir Philip Green warns of uncertain final quarter', *Retail Week*, 7 July 2009.

Manning, Clinton and Hiscott, Graham, 'Another good year for Topshop tycoon Sir Philip Green', *Daily Mirror*, 23 October 2009.

Mathiason, Nick, 'Where the rich stash their cash', *The Observer*, 27 March 2005.

Milligan, Lauren, 'Business is good', *Vogue*, 8 July 2009.

Milligan, Lauren, 'Arcadia up', *Vogue*, 22 October 2009.

Milligan, Lauren, 'European openings', *Vogue*, 23 October 2009.

Murphy, Richard, '"Sir" Philip Green – the rewards of tax avoidance', taxresearch.org.uk, 19 June 2006.

Nathan, Sara, 'Cowell to Phil his boots in TV deal', *The Sun*, 25 June 2009.

Peston, Robert, *Who Runs Britain?*, Hodder and Stoughton, 2008.

Randall, Jeff, 'The brilliant deal-doer behind Bhs', bbc.co.uk/business, 17 January 2002.

Robinson, James, '*The Observer profile:* Sir Philip Green: man with a fine attention to retail', *The Observer*, 28 June 2009.

Rushton, Suzie, 'Philip Green: The king of the high street in his most outspoken interview ever', *The Independent,* 5 July 2007.

Russell, Jonathan, 'Bono and Sir Philip Green go head to head', *The Daily Telegraph*, 4 November 2008.

Shields, Amy, 'Between a rock and a hard place', *Retail Week*, 5 June 2009.

Shields, Amy, 'Sir Philip Green warns against VAT level increases', *Drapers/Retail Week*, 10 June 2009.

The Sunday Times Rich List 2008, timesonline.co.uk.

Thurlow, Max, 'Sir Philip Green's girl Chloe blows her Topshop', *London Lite*, 17 September 2009.

Tomlinson, Richard, 'Kate Moss no guarantee Topshop beats US curse on UK chains', Bloomberg.com, 2 November 2009.

Vasagar, Jeevan, 'Pack your shorts, it's time for Sir Philip Green's birthday party', *The Guardian*, 12 March 2007.

Vernon, Polly, 'Three out of five women are in love with Philip Green. Well, his shops anyway', *The Observer*, 11 February 2007.

Wood, Zoe, 'Sir Philip Green names new chief executive of Arcadia store chain', *The Guardian*, 22 October 2009.

INDEX

LIZ BARCLAY

Liz Barclay is a freelance broadcaster, writer, communications trainer and business coach. She has presented various programmes on BBC Radio 4 for the past 11 years including the daily consumer programme *You and Yours* and the review programme *Pick of the Week*. She writes on business and personal finance for newspapers and magazines including the *Independent on Sunday*; has produced and presented 60 small business programmes for BBC 2; runs the website moneyagonyaunt.com and plans to launch a new site for SMEs in the spring of 2010. She has written several books including *Small Business Employment Law for Dummies* and is an experienced conference speaker and facilitator.